AESOP'S FABLES

Plays for Young Children

Dr. Albert Cullum

FEARON TEACHER AIDS

A Paramount Communications Company

Khanh Lee, the cover illustrator, is a 63-year-old artist from Saigon, Vietnam. Mr. Lee has lived in the United States for six months. He learned his craft from an older artist and mentor in his homeland.

Editorial Director: Virginia L. Murphy
Editor: Carolea Williams
Copyeditor: Kristin Eclov
Cover Illustration: Khanh Lee
Cover Design: Lucyna Green
Inside Illustration: Janet Skiles
Inside Design: Diann Abbott
Production: Rebecca Speakes

ISBN 0-86653-940-9

Printed in the United States of America
1. 9 8 7 6 5 4 3 2 1

CONTENTS

INTRODUCTION

Aesop's Fables provides students and teachers with a wide variety of short plays that can be easily performed by young children. No stage is needed and props are minimal. The plays require very little practice. Small groups of children will need approximately twenty minutes to prepare a play and five to ten minutes to perform it. The presentations can be followed by discussions that involve the entire class so that each student becomes a participant. Although the plays have been adapted from the fables of an early storyteller, Aesop presents many life problems that are still meaningful today. These dramatizations have been designed especially for use in kindergarten through third-grade classrooms.

Children seem to have a natural affinity for animals and can relate to their triumphs and foibles. Most of Aesop's fables are centered around animal characters. Children will easily relate to the situations and circumstances in which these characters find themselves. The performances encourage children to pantomime gestures and imitate the sounds and actions of familiar animals.

These quick and simple dramatizations also introduce children to a sense of formal theater without suppressing children's creativity. Perhaps one of the greatest things teachers can do for children is to give them opportunities to creatively express themselves. Through classroom drama, you will discover a uniqueness about your students—for they will share with you a delightful sense of humor, a remarkable sense of the dramatic, and a depth of emotion that may not surface during more structured classroom activities.

Theater has been a cultural element of many nations and races, beginning with the tribal storyteller and continuing to the most avant-garde theater of today. For centuries, people around the world have used theater as a release for emotions and tensions. I have discovered again and again in children from all backgrounds and walks of life that this type of release through theater can be extremely beneficial. Even if only for a moment, a child can soar like an eagle, chase an imaginary enemy around the desks of the classroom, or experience the thrill of an athletic victory.

During my many years of elementary-school teaching, I have yet to encounter a child who did not benefit by a touch of classroom theater. Classroom theater in its simplest form—without costumes, scenery, make-up, and lights—helps to establish a truly child-centered classroom. When children are allowed to be themselves, they see their own uniqueness. When they are given the opportunity to express their instinctive, intuitive sense of drama, they develop a sense of themselves.

CREATING POSITIVE EXPERIENCES

- Ask for volunteers to play each part. Never assign roles. There are two kinds of children—the ones who want the leading roles and the ones who are too sensitive or shy to pursue a leading character. Dramatics are not only for the obviously extroverted children, but also for the shy, quiet ones.

- The plays lend themselves naturally to a cooperative-learning environment. Encourage the characters in each short play to work together on their presentations. Invite students to read the dialogue together, make decisions about staging, and discuss inflection and tone of voice as they prepare for their performances.

- Respect student input and ideas. Presenting plays in the classroom can be a highly creative experience if the approach is child-centered. Don't concentrate on the final product as much as the process of getting there.

- Provide encouragement. Not only do you have the privilege of introducing great literature to young imaginative minds, but you have the priceless opportunity of giving children the gift of believing in themselves.

- Children who are able to read can use the reproducible play pages as scripts. Give these children copies of the scripts to practice with during independent time. Adult volunteers or older students can help younger children learn their parts. If children have difficulty memorizing their lines, encourage them to improvise.

- Limit props.

- Keep staging simple.

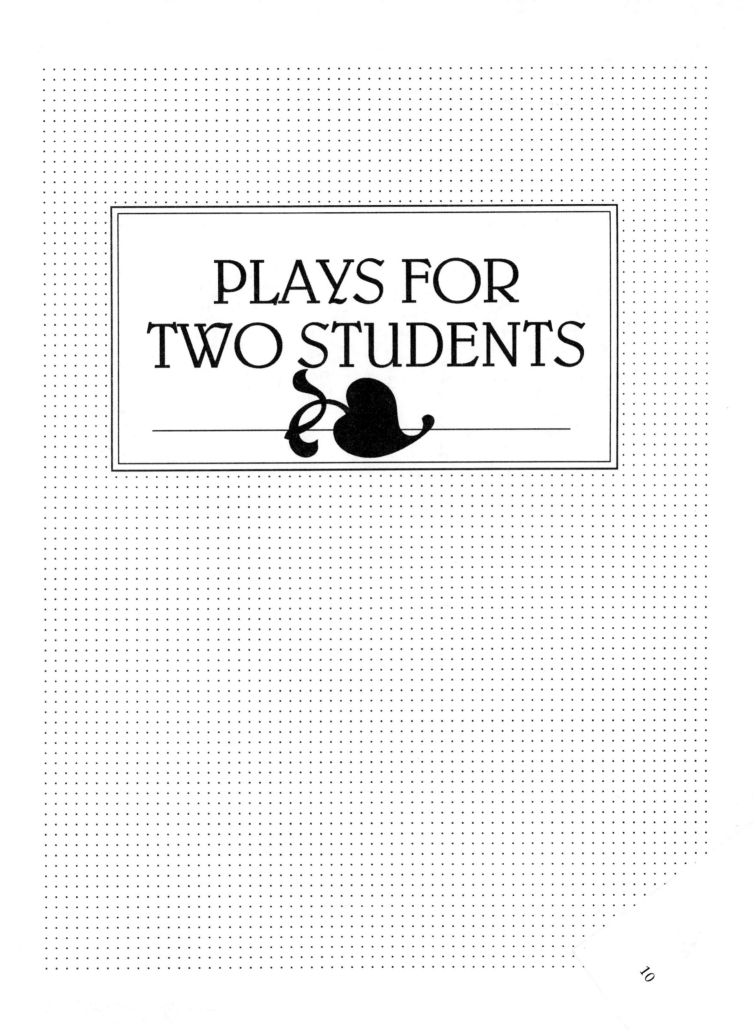

PLAYS FOR TWO STUDENTS

THE PEACOCK AND THE CRANE

Characters: Peacock
Crane

Staging: The story takes place along the edge of the woods. Invite the crane to "fly" about the entire room with imaginary widespread wings. Encourage the peacock to proudly walk around the entire room admiring his or her feathers.

Peacock: Everyone look at me! Look at my beautiful feathers! Look at my brilliant colors! Truly I am beautiful! Yes, I am the most beautiful bird in these woods! I am so beautiful that I am envied by all the other birds!

Crane: Are you still admiring yourself?

Peacock: And why not! I am robed as a king! Just look at the gold and purple in my feathers! Are they not just like the colors that a king wears?

Crane: Yes, they are pretty.

Peacock: Pretty you say? Pretty? I am magnificent! I have all the colors of the rainbow in my feathers.

Crane: Yes, you do have many colors.

Peacock: But poor you! You are so pale looking. You don't even have a tiny bit of color on your wings. You are so very, very pale. Poor you!

Crane: What you say about me is very true, Peacock. However, let me tell you something about myself that you might not know.

Peacock: What could you possibly have that would be better than anything I have?

Crane: I can do something that you can't do.

Peacock: And what is that?

Crane: I can fly up to the heavens and talk to the stars! All you can do is strut about on the ground. Keep your pretty feathers, Peacock. I will stay a bird who can fly!

> **Moral:** Everyone is special in his or her own way.

Aesop's Fables © 1993 Fearon Teacher Aids

THE WOLF AND THE MOUNTAIN GOAT

Characters: Wolf
Mountain Goat

Staging: The story takes place on a high cliff where a mountain goat is eating and a wolf is down below looking up. A chair can represent the mountain cliff. Encourage the wolf to speak in a very sweet voice.

Plays for Two Students

Wolf: This has been a bad day for me for I have not been able to catch one creature for my breakfast. I am very hungry! I wonder if I can convince that mountain goat to come down off her cliff to my level? Then I will pounce upon her! Hello, Goat! Say, can you hear me way up on your cliff?

Goat: Yes, I can hear you. What do you want, Wolf?

Wolf: Oh, I don't want anything. I was just worried about you way up there on your high cliff. Aren't you afraid that you might slip and fall?

Goat: I don't think I will fall.

Wolf: But if you do fall, you would break your leg. That would be a very painful injury, Goat!

Goat: Thank you for your concern, Wolf, but I'm perfectly safe up here.

Wolf: But the grass is much greener down here. Think of that.

Goat: The grass up here is good enough for me, Wolf.

Wolf: But the grass down here is the best grass in the world!

Goat: Thank you again. You are very kind to think about me.

Wolf: Are you sure you won't change your mind, Goat?

Goat: I'm quite sure that I won't change my mind.

Wolf: Why?

Goat: I know you too well, Wolf, to be tricked by you. You really don't care what I'm having for breakfast. You are only thinking about your own breakfast, and if I come down off my cliff, I will become your breakfast.

Wolf: Don't you trust me?

Aesop's Fables © 1993 Fearon Teacher Aids

Goat: Thank you again for your kind invitation, Wolf, but I don't think I will accept it.

> **Moral:** Don't believe everything that you hear.

THE MOUSE AND THE BULL

Characters: Mouse
                  Bull

Staging: The story takes place near a farmhouse. The hole in the farmhouse
               wall can be an opening of a large desk or a wastepaper basket.

Mouse: There is Bull sound asleep in the pasture. I think I will go and bite him on the leg!

(Slowly creeps up to the sleeping bull and gives him a sharp bite on his leg.)

Bull: Ouch! Ouch! That hurt! I'll get you back, Mouse!

(Chases the mouse, but the mouse runs safely into a small hole in the farmhouse.)

You can't hide from me, Mouse, for I am strong and powerful! I will knock down the wall to your little hole and eat you up!

(Snorts and snorts and then charges the wall, but all he does is hurt his head! Charges the wall again and again, and finally is so tired he stops.)

I know what I will do. I will rest right near your hole, Mouse, and catch you when you come out. I will wait all day just to get even with you. I am a strong and powerful bull and I can catch you!

(Waits and waits, but soon falls asleep and begins to snore.)

Mouse: Listen to Bull snore! I will sneak out of my hole very, very quietly and bite his leg again!

(Slowly creeps out of the hole and bites the bull very hard on the same leg, and then quickly scampers back to the safety of the hole.)

Bull: Ouch! Ouch! Ouch! That hurt!

(Goes back to the pasture crying about his bitten leg.)

Moral: Even little things can cause big problems.

Aesop's Fables © 1993 Fearon Teacher Aids

THE GRASSHOPPER AND THE OWL

Characters: Owl
Grasshopper

Staging: The story takes place in the daytime in the forest. The owl is resting in a hole in a tree and the grasshopper is on the grass below. Seat the owl on a chair. The owl can cover the grasshopper with a blanket or large piece of cloth at the end of the story.

Grasshopper: Chirp! Chirp! Chirp! Chirp! Chirp! Chirp! Chirp!

Owl: Grasshopper, may I ask a favor of you?

Grasshopper: Certainly. What favor?

Owl: As you know, I'm an owl. Owls stay awake all night and sleep all day, so would you mind going somewhere else to do your chirping. I am trying to rest.

Grasshopper: But I like chirping in this spot! Chirp! Chirp! Chirp! Chirp! Chirp! Chirp! Chirp! Chirp! Chirp!

Owl: Grasshopper!

Grasshopper: Yes, Owl?

Owl: This is a very, very big forest. Why can't you chirp somewhere else! Certainly in such a big forest there must be another spot where you feel comfortable.

Grasshopper: No, this is the only place in the whole forest that I like. Chirp! Chirp! Chirp! Chirp! Chirp! Chirp! Chirp! Chirp!

Owl: Grasshopper!

Grasshopper: Yes, Owl?

Owl: If this is the only place you like to chirp, then may I ask you another favor?

Grasshopper: Certainly, Owl. What is it?

Owl: Would you mind chirping with a very soft voice?

Grasshopper: No, I always chirp in a loud voice because my chirp is so beautiful! Chirp! Chirp! Chirp! Chirp! Chirp!

Owl: Grasshopper!

Grasshopper: Yes, Owl?

Owl: Come to think of it, you do have a lovely chirp. You probably have the most beautiful chirp in the whole forest.

Aesop's Fables © 1993 Fearon Teacher Aids

Grasshopper: Why, thank you Owl. How nice of you to say so.

Owl: Yes, I'm sure it's the most beautiful chirp in the whole world.

Grasshopper: Thank you, thank you, Owl. Chirp! Chirp! Chirp! Chirp! Chirp! Chirp! Chirp!

Owl: Since I cannot sleep because of your beautiful chirp, why don't you fly up to my hole in the tree and visit me. I have some delicious nectar that I will share with you. The delicious nectar will match the sweetness of your voice.

Grasshopper: Thank you, Owl. I accept your kind invitation.

(Flies up to the hollow of the tree where the owl gobbles him up.)

Moral: Don't be fooled by kind words.

THE WOLF AND THE HOUSE DOG

Characters: Wolf
Dog

Staging: The story takes place near a woods.

Plays for Two Students

Wolf: How wonderful you look! You are fat and sleek, while I am all skin and bones. I hunt day and night for food in these woods and most of the time I starve. How is it you don't have the same problem?

Dog: Well, I eat regularly everyday, and on holidays, I get extra treats!

Wolf: I still don't know what you are talking about!

Dog: I am fed every day because I guard my owner's house.

Wolf: You mean to say you get fed every day just for guarding your owner's house?

Dog: Very true! My owner treats me very nicely and pets me often. Come with me and I'll show you the house I guard.

Wolf: Yes, I would like to see the house you guard. But, say, what is that mark around your neck?

Dog: Oh that! That's nothing. That's the mark from the collar my owner places around my neck.

Wolf: You mean to tell me that you are not free to come and go as you like? You mean to tell me that you can't roam whenever and wherever you choose?

Dog: Not when my owner ties me up.

Wolf: Then good-bye my friend. I may be all skin and bones, but at least I'm free to come and go as I please.

> **Moral:** Some value freedom above all else.

Aesop's Fables © 1993 Fearon Teacher Aids

THE LION AND THE BULL

Characters: Lion
                     Bull

Staging: The story takes place near the edge of a forest. A wastepaper basket can represent the cooking pot. Encourage the lion and bull to stroll about the classroom on the way to the lion's den.

Lion: That's a beautiful bull in the pasture. I sure would like to have him for my dinner, but he's so big that I'm afraid to attack him. Perhaps I can trick him into coming into my cave where I'll have a better chance of capturing him.

(Moves toward the bull.)

Hello, Bull!

Bull: Hello, Lion. How are you today?

Lion: Fine, thank you. What are you doing?

Bull: Oh, just grazing. Why?

Lion: Well, I am having dinner and I thought you might like to come home and share my food with me. You will enjoy the meal.

Bull: Why are you asking me to share your dinner with you? Why don't you eat it all by yourself?

Lion: I'm asking you because you are my friend. Will you come?

Bull: Why, yes, I think I will.

(They walk into the forest to the entrance of the lion's den.)

Lion: Well, here we are at last. Why are you backing away, Bull?

Bull: I'm backing away because I don't see the dinner you promised. All I see is a large fire and a big pot. I have a feeling that I'm the dinner you are talking about.

Lion: I don't know what you're talking about.

Bull: I know what I'm talking about! Good-bye, Lion. Perhaps some other day I'll have dinner with you.

Moral: Look before you leap.

THE TWO FROGS

Characters: First Frog
Second Frog

Staging: The story takes place on a hot summer day. The two frogs are hopping along a dusty road. The long, dusty road can wind around the entire classroom. The well can be three or four desks placed close together with an opening in the center for the frog to jump into.

First Frog: We have been hopping along all day and I don't think we will ever find water! Every pond is all dried up!

Second Frog: Don't get discouraged! After all, this has been a very dry summer. Of course, it will take some time before we find a nice wet pond.

(The two frogs continue hopping down the dry dusty road.)

First Frog: Look! Look! There's a well! At last our journey is over!

(Both frogs jump to the edge of the well.)

Let's jump in! It looks so nice and wet!

Second Frog: Wait! Wait! Don't jump in!

First Frog: Don't be silly. Why not?

Second Frog: Let's talk about it first.

First Frog: There is nothing to talk about. All day long we have been hopping along this hot dusty road searching for water. Now we have found it, and you say, let's talk about it! I'm going to jump!

Second Frog: Wait a moment!

First Frog: I'm going to jump into the well right now!

Second Frog: Wait! Wait! Yes, the well is full of cool delicious water, but what if the well goes dry just like all the ponds? We would be in a dreadful situation—for we wouldn't be able to get out of the well!

First Frog: Don't be silly! The well isn't going to go dry.

Second Frog: You jump in if that's your decision. As for me, I'm going to keep hopping along the hot dusty road until I find a cool stream. Good-bye!

> **Moral:** Think about what you are going to do before you do it.

Aesop's Fables © 1993 Fearon Teacher Aids

THE FOX AND THE CROW

Characters: Fox
Crow

Staging: The story takes place in a forest. Use a chair as a branch for the crow to sit on.

Crow: Wow! I see a big piece of cheese that someone must have dropped accidentally. What luck! I will fly down and grab it.

(Flies down from the tree, snatches the piece of cheese, and flies back to the lofty branch.)

Fox: *(whispering)* Is that a Crow with a delicious piece of cheese in its mouth? I certainly would like to have that tasty piece of cheese for my breakfast! How can I get that piece of cheese from Crow? I don't know how to climb trees so I can't grab it. Even if I knew how to climb trees, Crow would fly away if I chased after her. The only way I can get the piece of cheese from Crow is by using my wits. My plan is to make Crow speak, then the piece of cheese will drop from Crow's mouth. *(loudly)* Good morning, Crow. Nice day today isn't it? How beautiful you look this bright early morn! Your eyes are so shiny! Your plumes look lovely in the morning sun. You know something? You are the most beautiful creature in the forest. Yes, you are! Tell me something. Can you sing? If I could only hear you sing, there would be no doubt in my mind at all. Then I would be certain that you were the finest bird in the world!

(The crow struts proudly up and down the branch.)

Yes, all crows are lovely, but you are the loveliest of them all. If you can sing as beautifully as you look, I'm sure you must be the most beautiful creature in the world.

Crow: Caw! Caw! Caw! Oh dear, I lost my lovely piece of cheese!

Fox: *(gobbling up the cheese)* Here is some good advice, Crow. Don't let sweet words fool you. Good-bye and thank you for the delicious piece of cheese.

(The crow cries and the fox shows great happiness and pride.)

Moral: Those who flatter often want something in return.

THE CHILD AND THE NUTS

Characters: Mother
Child

Staging: The story takes place in a house. Use an imaginary jar for the boy to reach his hand into.

Child: Mother, what are you carrying in the jar?

Mother: Some nuts. Would you like some?

Child: Oh yes, I love nuts! May I have as big a handful as I like?

Mother: You may have as big a handful as you can take.

(The child sticks his hands in the jar and grabs all the nuts a fist can hold.)

Child: But Mother, I can't get my hand out!

Mother: Let some of the nuts go and you will be able to pull your hand out.

Child: No! No! No! I want a big handful of nuts!

(Begins to cry because hand is stuck in the jar.)

Mother: There is no need to cry. Just let go of some of the nuts and your hand will come out.

Child: No! No! No! It's a mean old jar that won't let my hand go!

Mother: It's not the jar. It is you! You are being greedy!

Child: No! No! No! It's the jar's fault.

Mother: Listen, my child, be satisfied with half as many nuts and you will be able to get your hand out.

> **Moral:** Do not take more than you can carry.

THE FLEA AND THE OX

Characters: Flea
                   Ox

Staging: The story takes place in a barnyard. Encourage the flea to hop around a
                great deal. The ox should be peacefully resting, chewing his or her cud.

Flea: I really don't understand you, Ox!

Ox: What seems to be bothering you?

Flea: Well, here you are, big and strong, and yet you work hard for your owner day in and day out. You pull his wagons and plow his fields, even though you are big and strong and could tell him "No!"

Ox: Yes, I work hard for my owner.

Flea: Look at me, Ox! I'm very small and weak and yet I feed on your owner without doing any hard work!

Ox: I understand what you are saying, but I really don't mind working hard for my owner.

Flea: How can you say such a thing!

Ox: I am well fed by my owner, and he also likes me very much. Sometimes he even pats me on the head and tells me how good I am.

Flea: Oh dear! Oh dear! This patting on the head you like is bad for me. Whenever I get patted on the head, it brings about my destruction!

> **Moral:** Hard work is well rewarded.

Aesop's Fables © 1993 Fearon Teacher Aids

THE WILD BOAR AND THE FOX

Characters: Boar
                  Fox

Staging: The story takes place in the middle of a forest. A large table or desk can
               represent a sturdy tree trunk.

Boar: Now that I have a moment, I think I will sharpen my teeth. Here is a nice sturdy tree that will help me.

(Rubs and rubs his tusks against the very hard tree trunk.)

Fox: What in the world are you doing, Boar?

Boar: I'm sharpening my tusks.

Fox: That seems like a very silly thing to be doing.

Boar: Really! Why?

Fox: It's silly, for I don't see any danger about. I don't see a hunter and his dogs coming after you!

Boar: I don't see a hunter and his dogs coming after me, either.

Fox: Well, then, why all the nonsense about sharpening your tusks?

Boar: Fox, I don't think you understand. Wouldn't it be foolish of me to wait until the hunter and his dogs attacked before I sharpened my tusks? I think you are silly, not me!

Moral: Think ahead and be prepared.

Aesop's Fables © 1993 Fearon Teacher Aids

THE EAGLE AND THE HAWK

Characters: Eagle
                   Hawk

Staging: The story takes place in a high branch of a tree. Two chairs can represent the branch. Encourage the hawk to roam about the classroom in search of food.

Eagle: Oh! Oh! Oh dear! I feel so sad today! So very sad! Poor me!

Hawk: You look so sad today. Tell me why.

Eagle: *(sadly)* I have been looking for a companion for weeks, but no one will be my friend! Oh, poor me!

Hawk: Why don't you be my friend?

Eagle: You will be my friend?

Hawk: Sure, and if you promise to be my friend, I will supply you with much food every day.

Eagle: Are you sure you will be able to find food for me every day?

Hawk: Of course I'm sure, lovely Eagle. Why, just the other day I picked up a huge ostrich with my talons and carried him off into the sky!

Eagle: My, my! You must be a good hunter, Hawk!

Hawk: Yes, I'm sure I will be able to provide you with a good meal every single day. Yes, I'm very sure!

Eagle: Very well, Hawk, I will be your best friend! Now that we are good friends, fly off and bring me a huge ostrich, for I am hungry.

Hawk: Very well.

(Flies off but comes back with only a very little mouse.)

Eagle: You call that an ostrich? To me it looks like a very tiny mouse!

Hawk: Yes, I'm afraid that's all it is, a very tiny mouse.

Eagle: Is this the way you keep your promises?

Hawk: I was afraid you would not be my friend if I told you the truth!

Moral: Some people will promise anything to make a friend.

THE SEASIDE TRAVELERS

Characters: First Traveler
Second Traveler

Staging: The story takes place on a very high mountain overlooking the ocean. Two chairs can represent the mountain. When rushing down to the ocean, encourage the two travelers to make a long trip winding around the entire classroom.

Plays for Two Students

First Traveler: Look! Look! Isn't that something way out in the ocean?

Second Traveler: I wonder what it is?

First Traveler: It looks like a huge ship!

Second Traveler: Yes, it is a ship! Look how large the sails are!

First Traveler: It's a beauty of a ship!

Second Traveler: Let's go down to the harbor when it arrives.

First Traveler: It will be exciting to visit such a beautiful vessel!

Second Traveler: It's coming closer and I can see it better.

First Traveler: So can I, and it doesn't seem to be a huge ship at all!

Second Traveler: You are right! It doesn't have any sails!

First Traveler: You know what it is? It's just an old rowboat!

Second Traveler: How disappointing! It's just a rowboat drifting toward shore.

First Traveler: Let's rush down the mountain and see what's in it!

Second Traveler: Good idea! You know, we might find something valuable in a drifting rowboat!

First Traveler: Let's hurry down the mountain!

(The two travelers rush down the steep mountain running breathlessly to the edge of the water.)

Second Traveler: Another disappointment! It's only a bunch of large sticks tied together!

> **Moral:** Wishful thinking can be disappointing.

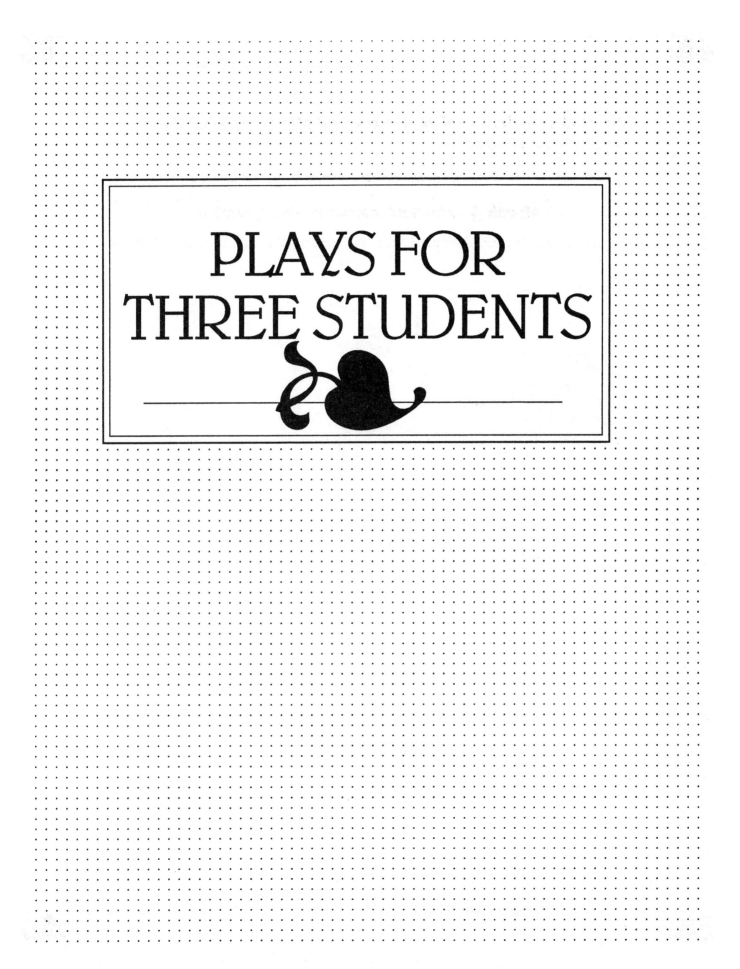

PLAYS FOR THREE STUDENTS

THE LION AND THE DOLPHIN

Characters: Lion
                  Dolphin
                  Bull

Staging: The story takes place near a seashore. The lion could stand on a table while the dolphin is pretending to swim on the floor.

Lion: Hello, Dolphin. Are you in the mighty ocean?

Dolphin: Yes, here I am, Lion. What is the matter?

Lion: Well, I have been thinking. I am king of the land, right?

Dolphin: Yes, you are correct.

Lion: And you are king of the ocean, correct?

Dolphin: Yes, you are correct, Lion.

Lion: Well, if I am king of the land and you are king of the ocean, we ought to be the best of friends.

Dolphin: I agree. Yes, let us be good friends.

Bull: I see a lion near the seashore. I think I will chase him.

(Charges toward the lion.)

Lion: Help! Help! Dolphin, help me! Help me, I pray!

Dolphin: Lion, I would like to help you, but my place is in the water. I am out of place and of no value on land.

Lion: You are a traitor! I thought we were the best of friends, and yet you refuse to help me against this bull.

Dolphin: You don't understand. I am not a traitor. If I could help you, I would, but, alas, nature did not give me the ability to live on land.

Moral: It's good to know what you can and cannot do.

Aesop's Fables © 1993 Fearon Teacher Aids

THE HERON

Characters: Heron
Perch
Catfish

Staging: The story takes place along the bank of a stream early one morning. Use a long piece of butcher paper to represent the stream. Encourage the heron to stroll proudly in the morning, but by nighttime, be quite tired and sad.

Plays for Three Students

Heron: What a beautiful morning. I think I'll go down to the stream and find myself a delicious breakfast. I want something very special this morning, not any old breakfast, but a breakfast fit for a king!

(Wanders down to the stream.)

Perch: Aren't you going to eat me for breakfast this morning, Heron?

Heron: Go away! You are much too small of a perch for me! Go away! This morning I want a breakfast fit for a king!

Catfish: Good morning, Heron.

Heron: Good morning and stop annoying me.

Catfish: But aren't you going to eat me for breakfast this morning?

Heron: Go away! Go away! Go away! You are much too bony. This morning I am looking for a breakfast fit for a king!

(Strolls up and down the stream.)

It is nearly noon, for the sun is way up in the sky, and I still don't have my breakfast.

(Continues to look, but finds nothing.)

It is beginning to get dark and I am very hungry, but I can't find a thing to eat. Poor me, not even a tiny minnow.

> **Moral:** One who is hard to please, may get nothing in the end.

THE HORSE AND THE DONKEY

Characters: Horse
Donkey
Horse's Owner

Staging: The story takes place along a country road. Encourage the donkey and horse to use the entire room. The horse should be very proud and full of energy. The donkey should be very old and weak.

Horse: Get out of my way you silly looking donkey!

Donkey: Can't you see I have heavy loads and that it is difficult for me to move quickly?

Horse: How dare you talk to me like that. You are nothing but an old donkey and I am a beautiful proud horse. Get out of my way!

Donkey: Yes. I will move out of your way, but give me time, for I am old and my load is heavy . . . very heavy!

Horse: Hurry, or I will kick you in the heels!

Donkey: I'm moving! I'm moving!

Horse: Watch me go right by you, you silly-looking donkey.

(Gallops by the donkey, flinging dust.)

Horse's Owner: *(the next day)* You know something, my dear horse? I think you are getting old and I should get myself a younger, more powerful horse!

Horse: Oh no, master! I am still a proud horse!

Horse's Owner: You were, but now you are not. I'm going to have you join the donkey and carry heavy loads. You will not have to run so fast anymore.

Donkey: Well, well, well! If it isn't the fine proud horse who made fun of me yesterday. Now, who can make fun of you?

> **Moral:** It is not good to make fun of others.

Aesop's Fables © 1993 Fearon Teacher Aids

THE PLAYFUL DONKEY

Characters: Donkey
                  Monkey
                  Donkey's Owner

Staging: The story takes place on the roof of a farmhouse. Encourage both the
               monkey and the donkey to do lively dancing.

Plays for Three Students

Monkey: Look at me, Donkey! Look at me! See how beautiful I can dance upon the rooftop.

Donkey's Owner: You are funny!

(Laughs loudly.)

Donkey: Yes, it seems to be a great deal of fun. I think I'll try it.

Monkey: I don't think you should try it, Donkey.

Donkey: Don't be silly. If you can do it, so can I. Perhaps even better!

Monkey: I wish you would change your mind.

Donkey: Out of my way! Watch me now!

(Begins to dance upon the rooftop. The shingles begin to fall off.)

Donkey's Owner: Get off that roof you foolish donkey! You are ruining my beautiful new roof!

Donkey: But when you saw the monkey dance on your roof, you thought it was very funny and you laughed and laughed.

Donkey's Owner: Get off, I say. You are ruining my roof. Get off now!

Donkey: But . . . .

Donkey's Owner: Never mind what the monkey did . . . get off immediately.

Moral: Don't do something just because others do.

THE BOY WHO WENT INTO THE RIVER

Characters: Child
Mother
Neighbor

Staging: The story takes place near a big river on a hot summer day. Use large pieces of cloth or a long piece of butcher paper to represent the river.

Mother: Listen carefully, my child. I don't want you swimming in the river while I'm away. Do you understand?

Child: Yes, Mother, I understand.

Mother: I will be back shortly. Good-bye, my child, and remember to obey me.

(Leaves.)

Child: It's such a hot day, I think I'll just wet my feet. Oh, that feels so good! I think I will go in, but just to my waist. Oooooh, that feels so good. I think I'll go in just up to my neck. Help! Help! Help! Help! The water is over my head and the current is so swift I can't get back to shore. Someone help me! Help! Help! Help! Help! Help me! I'm drowning!

Neighbor: You are a very careless young child for going into such deep water!

Child: I know! I know! But help me!

Neighbor: I'm sure you disobeyed your mother! Wait until she finds out!

Child: Yes, I disobeyed her, but help me! Help me!

Neighbor: Children are very foolish at times.

Child: Yes, but please help me first. Scold me afterwards!

> **Moral:** Give help first, then advice.

Aesop's Fables © 1993 Fearon Teacher Aids

Two Travelers and a Bear

Characters: First Traveler
Second Traveler
Bear

Staging: The story takes place along a path in the woods. Use a chair to represent a branch of the tree.

First Traveler: What a nice day to take a stroll through the woods. Aren't you glad you came along?

Second Traveler: Yes, you were a good friend to invite me.

First Traveler: Yes, I am your best friend!

(The bear growls loudly and stamps through the forest.)

Second Traveler: What was that noise?

First Traveler: Look over there! It's a huge bear!

Second Traveler: That bear is enormous and looks very angry.

First Traveler: Look, the bear sees us. It's starting to come this way.

Second Traveler: What shall we do?

First Traveler: I don't know what you are going to do, but I'm climbing up on this tree branch so the bear can't reach me.

Second Traveler: There are no other trees around with low branches. Where can I hide?

First Traveler: That's your problem. I know I'm safe from the bear. You will have to look after yourself. Sorry, my friend.

Second Traveler: I know what I will do. I will lie flat on the ground and pretend I am dead.

(The bear enters slowly growling loudly. He smells the body on the ground, then leaves.)

First Traveler: That certainly was a close call, but we both are safe.

Second Traveler: Yes, we both are safe.

First Traveler: For a moment I thought the bear was whispering something in your ear.

Second Traveler: Yes, the bear did whisper something in my ear.

Aesop's Fables © 1993 Fearon Teacher Aids

First Traveler: You're joking?

Second Traveler: No, I'm not joking. The bear told me to find another friend. He said I don't need friends like you.

Moral: Good friends won't leave you when you're in trouble.

Aesop's Fables © 1993 Fearon Teacher Aids

THE CROW AND MERCURY

Characters: Crow
Apollo
Mercury

Staging: The story takes place in a forest. The gods, Apollo and Mercury, could be standing high on a chair above the crow. The snare can be the legs of a classroom desk.

Crow: Help! Help me! Please someone help me! Can't someone see I am caught in a snare! Why doesn't someone help me! Where are all my friends when I need them? I know what I will do! I will call Apollo for help! Perhaps he will hear me and release me from this snare. Apollo, please look upon me with favor and release me from this powerful snare. Apollo, hear my plea! Please come and help me, Apollo! If you come and help me, I will hunt and hunt for the finest berries for you to eat.

Apollo: I heard your plea and I am here! If I release you from the snare, what will you promise me?

Crow: Apollo, I promise to bring you the finest berries of the forest for you to eat. I promise! I promise!

Apollo: Very well! I will now set you free from the snare.

(The crow immediately flies away, but soon is caught in another snare.)

Crow: I am trapped again! What shall I do! What shall I do! Help! Help! Someone come and help me. Poor me! I know what I will do! I will call Mercury for help. He will hear me and release me from this powerful snare. Mercury, come and help a poor little crow trapped in a powerful snare. Mercury, hear my plea. Please come and help me! I promise to hunt and hunt for the finest berries of the forest for you to eat if you will help me!

Mercury: I heard your plea, Crow. What is it you want me to do?

Crow: Please release me from this powerful snare.

Mercury: If I release you from the powerful snare, what will you promise to bring me?

Aesop's Fables © 1993 Fearon Teacher Aids

Crow: I promise to bring you the finest berries of the forest.

Mercury: Why should I believe you?

Crow: Because I made you a promise!

Mercury: But I heard you last week make the same promise to Apollo. And you never kept your promise.

Crow: Mercury, I will keep my promise this time!

Mercury: I do not believe you. I have decided not to release you from the powerful snare.

> **Moral:** It's hard to believe someone who doesn't keep a promise.

THE DOG, THE ROOSTER, AND THE FOX

Characters: Dog
Rooster
Fox

Staging: The story takes place in the middle of a woods. Use a chair to represent a tree.

Dog: Say, Rooster, let us take a long trip together.

Rooster: Good idea! Let's go.

(The dog and rooster start their trip.)

Dog: We have walked many miles and it is beginning to get dark. Don't you think we should find a place to sleep?

Rooster: Good idea. I will fly up to that high branch and sleep. Where will you sleep?

Dog: I'll sleep in the hole in the trunk.

Rooster: Sleep well. In the morning, we will continue our journey.

Dog: Good night, Rooster.

(Both the dog and rooster sleep soundly.)

Rooster: The sun is rising. I had better announce to the people that it is morning. Cock-a-doodle-do! Cock-a-doodle-do! Time to get up! Everybody up!

Fox: That is a fine rooster crowing. Perhaps this rooster will be my breakfast. Good morning, Rooster!

Rooster: Good morning, Fox.

Fox: Was that you I just heard crowing?

Rooster: Yes it was, Fox.

Fox: My, you have a beautiful voice! It is so loud and clear!

Rooster: Why thank you.

Fox: You crow so beautifully that I would like to be your friend.

Rooster: Why thank you.

Fox: Why don't you come down so we can have a chat?

Rooster: I have a better idea. Why don't you come up. Go around to the back of the tree to the hole in the trunk. Wake up my friend and he will let you in.

Fox: Thank you, Rooster. I know we are going to be great friends!

(The fox goes to the back of the tree, where the dog pounces upon him and scares him away.)

Moral: People who are not honest often get into trouble.

Aesop's Fables © 1993 Fearon Teacher Aids

THE GOOSE WHO LAID THE GOLDEN EGGS

Characters: Goose
Farmer
Farmer's Wife

Staging: The story takes place in a barnyard early one morning. Use the entire classroom for the goose chase.

Farmer: Time to go and gather the eggs. Where are you, my beautiful goose?

Goose: Here I am.

Farmer: How many eggs do you have for me this morning, my beautiful goose?

Goose: Just one as usual.

Farmer: But wait! What is this? Your egg this morning is yellow and very heavy. Is this some joke you are playing on me?

Goose: No. It is not a joke.

Farmer: But your egg this morning is of pure gold! Do you hear me? Pure gold!

Goose: Yes, I know.

Farmer: Wife! Wife! Come here quickly! Wife, come here quickly!

Wife: What are you yelling about?

Farmer: Look! Look! A solid golden egg!

Wife: Oh how wonderful! How wonderful!

Farmer: *(the next morning)* Time to go and gather the eggs. Where are you, my beautiful, beautiful, beautiful goose?

Goose: Here I am.

Farmer: How many eggs do you have for me this morning?

Goose: Just one as usual.

Farmer: I don't believe it! Another golden egg! Oh, you are a beautiful, beautiful goose!

Goose: Thank you.

Farmer: Wife! Wife! Come quickly!

Aesop's Fables © 1993 Fearon Teacher Aids

Plays for Three Students

Wife: Another golden egg! How lovely!

Farmer: *(whispering to his wife)* Why should we wait every morning for a golden egg from our beautiful goose. If we cut the goose open, we will get all the golden eggs at once and we will be rich, rich, rich!

Goose: I heard you! You wouldn't do that to me would you? Remember, I'm your beautiful goose. Remember?

Farmer: I want all of your golden eggs now. Now!

(Begins to chase the goose around the barnyard.)

Now I have you.

(Cuts the goose open.)

Oh no! My beautiful goose is not full of golden eggs. Oh no! What have I done!

> **Moral:** A person who is too greedy may end up with nothing.

THE CAT AND THE MONKEY

Characters: Cat
Monkey
Owner of the House

Staging: The story takes place on a very cold day. The cat and monkey are sitting in front of the fireplace. The opening of a large desk makes an ideal fireplace. Use a wastepaper basket for the cat to quickly flip chestnuts out of for the monkey to catch in the air.

Plays for Three Students

Monkey: The fire makes us feel so warm. And you look splendid sitting in front of the fireplace.

Cat: Thank you, Monkey.

Monkey: Those chestnuts roasting in the fireplace smell so good.

Cat: Yes, they certainly do.

Monkey: I'm sure they taste good, too. Wouldn't it be nice to eat some of them?

Cat: Yes, it would, but how can we get them out of the fire?

Monkey: You are so clever at such things, you good-looking cat. You are much more clever than I am!

Cat: Oh thank you, Monkey.

Monkey: Why don't you pull some chestnuts out of the fire and we will eat them!

Cat: But I'm afraid of burning my delicate paws!

Monkey: Oh, but you are so nimble and quick. You won't burn your beautiful little paws.

Cat: Very well, I will pull out the chestnuts for us to eat.

(Begins to pull out chestnuts from the fire, but as quickly as the nuts are pulled out, the monkey eats them.)

My paw is getting burned and it hurts me!

Monkey: But you are doing very well! Keep trying!

Owner: Get away from the fireplace and stop eating my chestnuts. You both are very naughty.

(The monkey and cat scamper to another part of the house.)

Aesop's Fables © 1993 Fearon Teacher Aids

Cat: My paw is very burned and I didn't even get one chestnut to eat! You ate them all, Monkey! Next time I'll know better. I won't pull any more chestnuts out of the fire for you!

> **Moral:** Beware of those who flatter, for they usually want something in return.

Aesop's Fables © 1993 Fearon Teacher Aids

Plays for Three Students

THE DOVE AND THE ANT

Characters: Ant
Dove
Hunter

Staging: The story takes place in a meadow during a hot afternoon. The dove can perch on a classroom chair. Use a long piece of butcher paper to represent the brook.

Ant: I'm so thirsty. I think I will go down to the brook for a drink of cool water.

(At the brook, the ant accidentally falls in.)

Help! Help! Help! Help! Someone save me! Help!

Dove: *(sitting in a nearby tree)* Poor little ant. What can I do to help? I know! I'll drop a leaf into the brook. The ant can use the leaf as a raft to get to shore.

(Drops the leaf into the brook and the ant is saved.)

Ant: Thank you, kind dove.

(A hunter is creeping close to the tree.)

Hunter: *(whispering)* Look at that beautiful dove in the tree. I'll spread my net and snare him.

Ant: Oh, no you don't! That dove saved me from drowning and I will not allow you to catch him in your net, Hunter.

(Bites the hunter on the leg.)

Hunter: Ouch!

(The dove is startled by the noise and swoops away to safety.)

Moral: One good deed leads to another.

Aesop's Fables © 1993 Fearon Teacher Aids

THE WIND AND THE SUN

Characters: Wind
Sun
Human Being

Staging: The story takes place in an open field. Encourage the wind to use a fan or just blow air from his or her mouth when huffing and puffing. Invite the sun to hold up a piece of bright yellow paper to send out heat.

Wind: Sun, you are so silly to say that you are stronger and more powerful than I am.

Sun: But my dear Wind, you are foolish not to realize that what I say is very true!

Wind: But my dear Sun, everybody, yes everybody, knows that I am stronger!

Sun: I don't believe what everybody says. People are very often mistaken.

Wind: You really make me laugh the way you talk. How could anyone or anything be stronger than the wind?

Sun: Yes, I agree that you are strong, but all I say is that you are not as strong as I am.

Human Being: Will you two stop arguing. You are keeping me awake and I have much work to do tomorrow.

Wind: It's all the sun's fault!

Human Being: There you go again with your foolish arguing. Tomorrow we will have a contest between you two. I will wear my heavy cloak and the one that makes me take my cloak off will be the champion. Fair enough?

Wind: Yes.

Sun: Yes.

Human Being: Good! Now go to sleep so I can rest, and we will meet in the open field tomorrow at noon. Good night.

(The next day.)

Are the two of you ready?

Wind: Yes.

Sun: Yes.

Aesop's Fables © 1993 Fearon Teacher Aids

Human Being: Good. I have on my heavy cloak. Wind, you will go first to see if you can make me take off my heavy cloak.

Wind: Get ready, for soon you will be without a cloak.

(Huffs and puffs and huffs and puffs, but the human being wraps the cloak more tightly around him.)

Oh dear, I'm all out of breath! I'm all out of wind, and I failed to remove the cloak.

Human Being: All right, your turn, Sun.

Sun: I'm ready.

(Begins to shine brightly upon the human being and soon he feels so hot he removes the cloak.)

Human Being: You win, Sun. You are the champion!

Moral: People respond better to kindness than force.

THE HARE AND THE TORTOISE

Characters: Hare
Tortoise
Fox

Staging: The story takes place in a woods. Make a race track that circles the entire room. Use a chair to represent a mountain peak.

Hare: Ha-ha-ha-ha-ha-ha-ha! My dear Tortoise, please forgive me for laughing, but I can't help it. Ha-ha-ha-ha-ha-ha-ha!

Tortoise: What are you laughing at?

Hare: Ha-ha-ha-ha-ha-ha-ha! Your legs! Ha-ha-ha-ha-ha-ha!

Tortoise: What is so funny about my legs?

Hare: They are so short! Ha-ha-ha-ha-ha-ha-ha! And you travel so slowly! You are truly a funny sight! Ha-ha-ha-ha-ha!

Tortoise: I'm glad you are so amused, but let me tell you this. Even though you are as swift as the wind, I can beat you in a race.

Hare: What did you say?

Tortoise: I said I can beat you in a race!

Hare: Ha-ha-ha-ha-ha-ha-ha-ha-ha!

Tortoise: Are you afraid to accept my challenge?

Hare: Afraid? Ha-ha-ha-ha-ha-ha-ha-ha! You truly are a fool. You are so slow and I am so fast. How could you possibly win a race?

Tortoise: We will never know unless we try it.

Hare: Ha-ha-ha-ha-ha-ha!

Tortoise: Why don't you stop laughing so we can race.

Hare: Ha-ha-ha-ha-ha-ha! All right, I accept your challenge. Now, who will decide what course we run?

Tortoise: Perhaps Fox over there will plan the course for us?

Fox: What can I do for you?

Hare: This silly tortoise has challenged me to run a race. Will you decide what course we are to run?

Aesop's Fables © 1993 Fearon Teacher Aids

Fox: Certainly, glad to be of help. The course you will run will be the road that leads directly up the mountain. The one who reaches the peak first is the winner.

Tortoise: Fair enough.

Hare: I'm ready, Tortoise, are you? Ha-ha-ha-ha-ha-ha!

Tortoise: Yes, I'm ready.

Fox: Get ready! On your mark! Get set! Go!

(The race begins. The hare quickly runs far ahead and the tortoise is left way behind.)

Hare: This is a silly, silly race. I'm so far ahead I can't even see the poor Tortoise. I think I'll take a little nap in this cool grass.

(The hare falls sound asleep. The tortoise continues at his slow pace, quietly goes by the hare, and reaches the peak of the mountain first.)

Well, that was a nice nap. I still don't see that silly tortoise. Ha-ha-ha-ha-ha-ha-ha-ha-ha-ha! Well, might as well go to the peak of the mountain and wait for the tortoise there. Ha-ha-ha-ha-ha-ha!

(The hare strolls leisurely to the peak of the mountain where he finds the tortoise waiting.)

Tortoise: Hello, dear Hare! Where have you been? You see, I told you I could beat you in a race and I have!

> **Moral:** Slow, but steady, wins the race.

Aesop's Fables © 1993 Fearon Teacher Aids

THE CITY MOUSE AND THE COUNTRY MOUSE

Characters: City Mouse
Country Mouse
Dog

Staging: The story begins in the home of the country mouse and then moves to the home of the city mouse. Encourage the actors to use the entire room when traveling from the country to the city. Prepare a large dinner table. Encourage the mice to explore the table in detail.

Country Mouse: My dear cousin from the city, how nice of you to come all this way to visit me.

City Mouse: I'm glad to be here, although I will admit it was a long journey.

Country Mouse: Please make yourself at home while I prepare dinner.

City Mouse: Thank you, my country cousin.

Country Mouse: Let's have our dinner outside underneath the big tree. The air smells so good, and we can relax there. Is that all right with you?

City Mouse: Anything you say cousin.

(They carry the food outside and sit under a big tree.)

Now, here is what we shall have to eat. Some bread, some cheese, some bacon, some beans, and for dessert, we will go searching for some acorns.

City Mouse: Thank you, country cousin, but how can you put up with such poor food as this?

Country Mouse: Don't you like it? I think it's delicious!

City Mouse: But the bread is moldy, the cheese is hard, and the bacon and beans are dry!

Country Mouse: I'm sorry you don't like it, but that's all I have to offer.

City Mouse: I have a wonderful idea! Why don't you come to the city with me? There we can eat all kinds of delicious food, and for dessert, we can have some very sweet cookies.

Country Mouse: Very well, I will go to the city with you.

(The two mice begin their long trip to the city.)

Aesop's Fables © 1993 Fearon Teacher Aids

City Mouse: Here we are! Look! The people who live here have not cleared the table and have left much food. Look at all the things we can eat!

Country Mouse: I don't believe what I see! Is it all real? All this food!

City Mouse: Yes, it's all real. I eat this way every night. Try some of the sweet grapes, the soft cheese, the nuts, the pudding, and the crackers. And for dessert, we can eat the sweet tasty jelly.

Country Mouse: You are right, my city cousin, your food is much better.

(In another room a huge dog starts barking.)

What was that?

City Mouse: Hurry! Hurry! We have to leave quickly for that noise means danger!

(The two mice scamper off the table and hide in a little hole in the wall. The dog enters barking and sniffs at the hole but finally goes away.)

I think it's safe to go back and finish our dinner.

Country Mouse: No thank you, my city cousin.

City Mouse: What are you doing?

Country Mouse: I'm preparing to go back to my country home.

City Mouse: You mean right now, with all that food still left on the table?

Country Mouse: I'm leaving right now . . . this very minute!

City Mouse: But I don't understand!

Country Mouse: Let me explain, dear city cousin. Yes, I agree your food is much better and tastier than mine, but I don't enjoy eating and wondering when that dog is going to hear us and rush back in. Good-bye, dear city cousin. I'm going back to the peace and quiet of the country where I won't have to worry about angry dogs.

Moral: Better safe than sorry.

Aesop's Fables © 1993 Fearon Teacher Aids

Plays for Three Students

THE MISER

Characters: Miser
                    Worker
                    Neighbor

Staging: The story takes place at the home of a miser on the outskirts of a town.

Miser: I have sold all my furniture, my dishes, and my clothes for this beautiful, beautiful, beautiful lump of gold! Look how it shines! Isn't it magnificent? Yes, and it's all mine! All my very own! . . . Now comes my problem. Where shall I hide my beautiful lump of gold? Where? Where? Where? Let me think . . . . Yes, I'll bury it in my backyard.

(Digs a deep, deep hole and buries the lump of gold in the middle of the night so no one will see.)

Miser: *(the next day)* Is my gold safe? I had better check to see if it is still safe. Suppose someone has stolen it. Oh, I'm so worried!

(Digs up the gold.)

Thank heavens it is safe! Now to bury it again. I don't think anyone saw me. I'm sure no one saw me.

(Goes back into the house.)

Worker: I wonder why that old miser keeps digging a hole in the backyard and then covering it up. I'm very curious. I think I'll check to see what is buried in that hole.

(Digs up the hole and discovers the lump of gold.)

Why it's a lump of gold! I think I'll keep it!

(Runs away with the lump of gold.)

Miser: I had better check my lump of gold to see if it is safe. Oh no! Oh no! Oh no! My lump of gold is gone! Help! Help! Help! Someone has stolen my lump of gold! Help! Help!

Neighbor: Why are you crying so?

Miser: Someone has stolen my lump of gold. It's gone! Gone! Gone! Do you hear me . . . it's gone!

Neighbor: Don't be so unhappy.

Miser: Are you crazy? My lump of gold is gone and you are telling me not to be so unhappy!

Aesop's Fables © 1993 Fearon Teacher Aids

Neighbor: No, I'm not crazy and I'll tell you why. Place a stone in the hole and pretend it is your precious lump of gold.

Miser: You don't make sense!

Neighbor: I make great sense. The stone will be as valuable as your lump of gold, for you are not spending your gold when you bury it in the ground. So, pretend the lump of stone is a lump of gold.

Moral: You can't miss what you don't have.

THE GNAT AND THE LION

Characters: Gnat
                  Lion
                  Spider

Staging: The story takes place in the middle of a forest. The spider's web can be a
               large cobweb drawn on the chalkboard.

Plays for Three Students

Gnat: Well, well, well if it isn't Lion.

Lion: Get away from me you silly little gnat. You are nothing but a nuisance!

Gnat: I am not afraid of you and I don't think you are stronger than I am!

Lion: Go away and let me get my rest.

Gnat: All you can do is scratch with your claws and bite with your teeth. I repeat, I am stronger than you!

Lion: Are you still here? Go away!

Gnat: Don't be so sure of yourself, Lion. Come, I'll challenge you to a fight to prove to you that I am stronger than you.

Lion: Very well! Anything to shut you up.

(The gnat begins to buzz about the lion, stinging him on the nose, on his tail, in his ear, and on his head. The poor lion finally gives up trying to slap the gnat with his paw.)

Yes, you win, you pesky little gnat!

Gnat: I told you so! I told you so!

(Buzzes about the forest feeling very proud and bragging to every-one.)

Look at me everyone! The lion thought he was the king of the forest, but I showed him! Yes, he may be bigger than I am and have sharper claws, but I defeated him. He admitted, himself, that I won the fight. How powerful I am! I'm stronger than the lion!

(Runs into a spider's web and is trapped.)

Spider: Well, well, well, well, my little gnat. I have you trapped in my web.

Aesop's Fables © 1993 Fearon Teacher Aids

Gnat: Help! Help! Help!

Spider: No one hears you my little gnat. The more you struggle the more you are trapped!

Gnat: Poor me! How is it that I can defeat the powerful lion, but I am helpless against a weak spider? Poor me!

Spider: And now, my little gnat, I am going to have a delicious meal by eating you up!

(Gobbles up the little gnat.)

Moral: You can always find someone bigger or stronger.

Aesop's Fables © 1993 Fearon Teacher Aids

THE CRAB AND THE FOX

Characters: First Crab
Second Crab
Fox

Staging: The story begins near the seashore and moves inland to a meadow.

First Crab: I'm tired of living near and in the water. I'm always so damp and cold. Let's move somewhere else.

Second Crab: Where do you have in mind, cousin crab?

First Crab: The meadow looks like a nice place to live. It looks so green and smells so good.

Second Crab: But don't you think that would be a dangerous place for us to live?

First Crab: Don't be so frightened of everything. Why couldn't we live there?

Second Crab: Something tells me that it's best that we stay near the water.

First Crab: I don't care what you say, my dear cousin. I'm moving to the beautiful fresh meadow.

Second Crab: Good luck, cousin, but I'm staying here where I belong.

(The first crab slowly makes his way to the meadow.)

First Crab: Oh, it smells so good! I'm so glad I left my watery home, so very glad!

Fox: Well, well, well . . . what do we have here in the meadow?

First Crab: Fox, you aren't going to harm me are you?

Fox: I'm going to eat you up for my dinner, little crab!

First Crab: Oh no! Why did I ever leave my seashore home? Yes, I deserve this fate!

(The fox hovers over the crab, waiting to pounce on it.)

> **Moral:** Be happy where you are.

Aesop's Fables © 1993 Fearon Teacher Aids

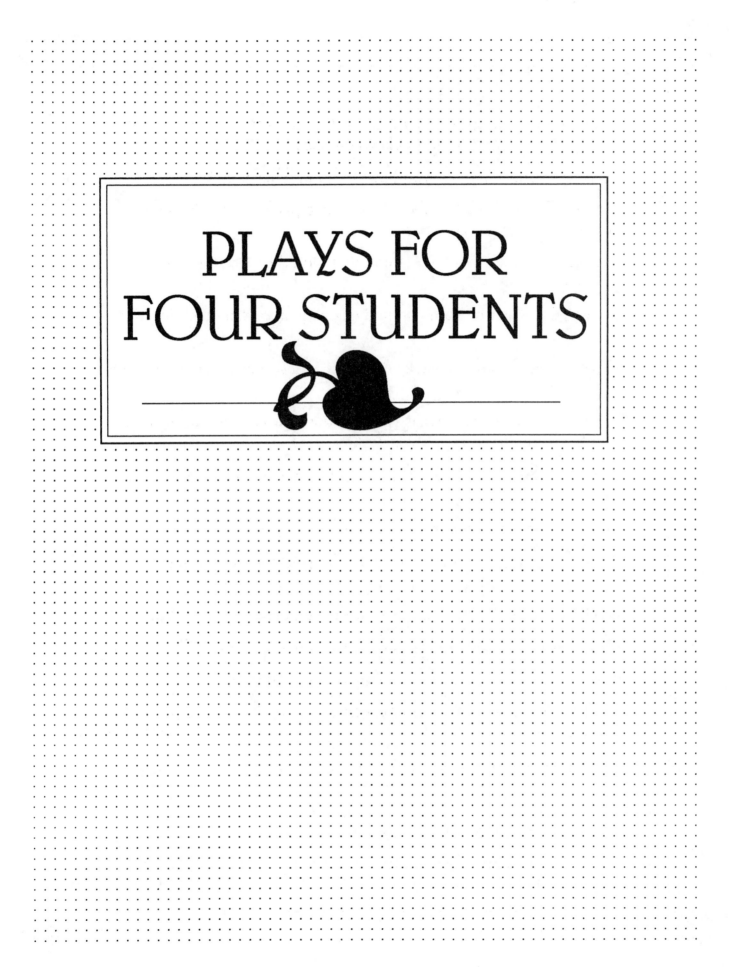

PLAYS FOR FOUR STUDENTS

THE MOTHER LARK AND HER BABIES

Characters: Mother Lark   Second Baby Lark
First Baby Lark   Farmer

Staging: This story takes place early one morning in a nest in the middle of a wheat field. Encourage the larks to sit under a table that represents their nest.

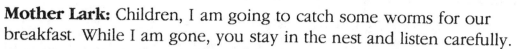

Mother Lark: Children, I am going to catch some worms for our breakfast. While I am gone, you stay in the nest and listen carefully.

First Baby Lark: What should we listen for, Mother?

Mother Lark: Listen and see if you can find out when the wheat field is going to be cut, for we will have to move our nest before that happens.

Second Baby Lark: We will listen carefully, Mother.

(The mother lark flies away. The farmer enters.)

Farmer: I think I will ask my neighbors to help me cut the wheat field today.

First Baby Lark: Did you hear that?

Second Baby Lark: Yes, I heard.

(The mother lark flies back.)

Mother Lark: Well, what did you hear my little ones?

First Baby Lark: Oh Mother, Mother, the farmer is asking his neighbors to help him cut the wheat field today!

Second Baby Lark: We had better move our nest now, Mother!

Mother Lark: Don't be alarmed, my little ones. There is no need to move our nest today. Now, open your mouths for here are the worms I promised to find for you.

First Baby Lark: Thank you, Mother.

Second Baby Lark: Thank you, Mother.

Mother Lark: *(the next day)* I am going to catch some worms for your breakfast. While I am gone, listen carefully.

First Baby Lark: We will listen carefully, Mother.

Second Baby Lark: We will listen very carefully, Mother.

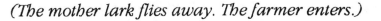

(The mother lark flies away. The farmer enters.)

Farmer: I think I will ask my friends to help me cut my wheat field today.

First Baby Lark: Did you hear that?

Second Baby Lark: Yes, I heard it!

(The mother lark flies back.)

Mother Lark: What did you hear, my little ones?

First Baby Lark: Oh, Mother, let us hurry away now!

Second Baby Lark: Yes Mother, let us hurry away, for the farmer is asking his friends to help him cut the wheat field today!

Mother Lark: No need to worry, my little ones, for the wheat field won't be cut today. Open your mouths for here are the worms I promised you.

First Baby Lark: Thank you, Mother.

Second Baby Lark: Thank you, Mother.

Mother Lark: *(the third day)* I am going to catch some worms for your breakfast. Listen carefully while I am gone.

First Baby Lark: We will listen carefully, Mother.

Second Baby Lark: We will listen carefully, Mother.

(The mother lark flies away. The farmer enters.)

Farmer: I think I will cut the wheat myself today.

First Baby Lark: Did you hear what I heard?

Second Baby Lark: I certainly did hear what you heard!

(The mother lark flies back.)

Mother Lark: Well, what did you hear today, my little ones?

Aesop's Fables © 1993 Fearon Teacher Aids

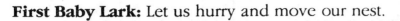

First Baby Lark: Let us hurry and move our nest.

Second Baby Lark: Yes, Mother, let us hurry and move our nest, for we heard the farmer say he is going to cut the wheat field himself today.

Mother Lark: Yes, my little ones, we must hurry and move our nest, for today the wheat field surely will be cut. When one does not depend on anyone else for help, the job will get done.

Moral: If you want something done, do it yourself.

PEACOCK AND JUNO

Characters: Peacock   Nightingale
                  Juno   Owl

Staging: The story takes place near a forest. Juno can be just a voice or a character
               that appears in person.

Owl: Sing us another pretty song, Nightingale, for you have such a lovely voice.

Nightingale: Thank you for the compliment, Owl.

(Bursts into song—whistling, humming, and singing.)

Owl: Yes, you truly have a most delicate voice. Thank you, Nightingale, for making all the creatures of the forest so happy with your song.

Peacock: I, too, have a nice voice!

(Attempts to sing, but can only make ugly, harsh sounds.)

Owl: Ha-ha-ha-ha-ha-ha-ha-ha-ha-ha! When you sing, you are the laughingstock of the forest, Peacock. I suggest that you never attempt to sing again. I think it best that you parade about and show everyone your beautiful plumage.

(Flies away.)

Peacock: Why don't I have a beautiful voice? I, too, would love to make all the creatures of the forest happy with my voice. I'm so unhappy that I can't sing!

Juno: Don't be so unhappy, Peacock. It is true that you can't sing like Nightingale, but you are far more beautiful. Your feathers are the talk of the forest.

Peacock: But what good is my beauty if I can't sing?

(Begins to cry.)

Juno: There, there . . . don't cry, Peacock, for it was decided a long time ago that each creature of the forest would be noted for certain things. For example, the nightingale would be famous for song, the eagle for strength, and you, Peacock, for your beauty. Now, let me see you spread your wings and walk proudly.

Aesop's Fables © 1993 Fearon Teacher Aids

Peacock: Oh very well, I'll strut about and show my plumage to all the creatures of the forest.

(Proudly struts about.)

> **Moral:** Each person has his or her own special qualities.

Aesop's Fables © 1993 Fearon Teacher Aids

THE DOGS AND THE HIDES

Characters: Black Dog   Brown Dog
White Dog   Spotted Dog

Staging: The story takes place near a big river. A large piece of cloth or a blanket can represent the river. As each dog floats away, a member of the audience can carefully drag the blanket along the floor.

Black Dog: See those big poles sticking out of the middle of the river?

White Dog: Yes, I see them. What are they?

Black Dog: They are poles. And attached to those poles are some delicious hides!

Brown Dog: That makes me extra hungry! Let's go and get them.

Spotted Dog: Don't be silly. How can we get them when the water in the middle of the river is deep and swift?

Brown Dog: What shall we do then? I'm very hungry!

White Dog: I am very hungry, too!

Black Dog: I know how we can get to the hides.

Spotted Dog: Tell us! Tell us!

White Dog: Hurry and tell us!

Brown Dog: Yes, hurry, for I'm starving!

Black Dog: We can drink up all the water in the river.

Spotted Dog: That's a wonderful idea!

White Dog: Do you really think we can drink up all the water? There's a great deal of water in that river.

Black Dog: Of course we can drink up all the water in the river—if we all work together. Now let's get started.

(The four dogs start drinking and drinking and drinking.)

White Dog: Oh dear ! Oh dear! I'm so full of water I'm going to float away!

(The white dog floats down the river out of sight.)

Spotted Dog: Look! Look! The white dog is floating away!

Aesop's Fables © 1993 Fearon Teacher Aids

Black Dog: Don't worry about him. That just means there will be more of the hides for us.

Brown Dog: Oh dear! Oh dear! I'm so full of water I'm going to float away!

(The brown dog floats down the river out of sight.)

Spotted Dog: Look! Look! The brown dog is floating away!

Black Dog: Don't worry about him. That just leaves the two of us to split the hides. That means more for both of us!

Spotted Dog: Oh dear! Oh dear! I'm so full of water that I'm going to float away, too! Help me! Help me! Help! Help!

Black Dog: I'm not going to help you, for now the hides are all for me!

(The spotted dog floats away out of sight.)

I must now finish drinking the water in the river and then I will be able to eat the delicious hides all by myself.

(Drinks and drinks and drinks.)

I'm almost finished. Just a few more gallons and then I'll eat the hides . . . the delicious hides! I can hardly wait!

(Drinks and drinks and finally becomes so full of water that he, too, floats away!)

Moral: Greedy behavior will only get you in trouble!

Aesop's Fables © 1993 Fearon Teacher Aids

THE OX AND THE FROG

Characters: First Little Frog   Third Little Frog
Second Little Frog   Mother Frog

Staging: The story takes place in a little pond in the middle of a woods. Chairs for the audience can be placed in a circle to suggest a pond in the middle. On three rocks in the center of the pond sit three little frogs. The mother frog can get bigger and bigger by starting on the floor, then moving to a chair, and finally to a table.

First Little Frog: Oh Mother! Oh Mother!

Second Little Frog: Mother, where are you!

Third Little Frog: Mother, come quickly!

Mother Frog: Coming children.

First Little Frog: Hurry, Mother! Hurry!

Mother Frog: Now, what is all this excitement about?

First Little Frog: We have just seen a most frightening monster!

Second Little Frog: He was as big as a tall, tall tree!

Third Little Frog: He had a long, long tail and long pointed horns!

Mother Frog: There is no reason to be frightened, my children. That was just an ox. Yes, the ox was big, but not much bigger than I am. Now you watch children. I'm going to huff and puff and make myself as big as the ox you saw.

(Huffs and puffs to make herself big.)

Now, children, am I just as big as the ox?

First Little Frog: Oh no, Mother!

Second Little Frog: Oh no, Mother!

Third Little Frog: Oh no, Mother! The ox was much, much bigger!

Mother Frog: Then I will try again. Now watch me children.

(Huffs and puffs and huffs and puffs.)

Now children, certainly I must be as big as the ox!

First Little Frog: Oh no, Mother!

Second Little Frog: Oh no, Mother!

Third Little Frog: Oh no, Mother. The ox was much, much bigger!

Mother Frog: Very well, I will try again. Now watch me, children.

(Huffs and puffs and huffs and puffs and huffs and puffs and finally falls over, exhausted.)

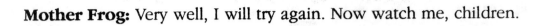

Moral: Don't try to be something that you're not.

Aesop's Fables © 1993 Fearon Teacher Aids

THE GOAT AND THE DONKEY

Characters: Goat   Farmer
           Donkey   Doctor

Staging: The story takes place on a farm. The goat and the donkey can stand on chairs from which the donkey jumps.

Goat: I am very jealous of all the delicious food the donkey is given, while all I have is scraps and things I find for myself. Perhaps I can play a trick on him so there will be more food for me.

(The donkey wanders by.)

Donkey: Hello, Goat. You seem to be very sad today. What is the matter?

Goat: I was feeling very sorry for you.

Donkey: Feeling sorry for me? Why? I'm very happy on this farm. My owner treats me very well. Don't feel sorry for me, Goat.

Goat: But I do! I do! The farmer is not treating you well at all! Look how hard the farmer makes you work at the mill!

Donkey: I never thought of it that way.

Goat: And, also, look at the heavy burden the farmer makes you carry each day back and forth from the mill.

Donkey: Yes, you are right! I do work very hard. What do you suggest I do to make my life easier?

Goat: I have a wonderful idea! Why don't you pretend to have a fainting spell and fall into the ditch. Then your owner will have to give you a long rest.

Donkey: That's a great idea! Thank you, Goat. Thank you very much.

(Jumps into a ditch and is hurt by the fall.)

Farmer: Help! Help! Help! My wonderful donkey has fallen into a ditch! Help! Help! Someone come and help.

Doctor: I am a doctor. May I be of help?

Farmer: Oh yes, yes! Look! My wonderful donkey, my loyal donkey, has fallen into a ditch and seems to be close to death! What can I do?

Aesop's Fables © 1993 Fearon Teacher Aids

Doctor: Let me think. Let me think. I think the best way to save your wonderful donkey is to toss a goat into the ditch as well. I'm sure that will help him recover.

Farmer: Thank you, doctor, thank you. I will do just that.

Goat: Oh no! My idea has backfired! Oh no!

(The goat, hearing the words of the doctor, begins to run away as the farmer chases close behind.)

Moral: Selfish plans often have unhappy endings.

Aesop's Fables © 1993 Fearon Teacher Aids

THE WOLF AND THE CRANE

Characters: Wolf   Rabbit
                  Crane   Donkey

Staging: The story takes place in a woods one morning.

Wolf: Oh my, this is a delicious dinner. Yes, yes! Very, very tasty! Oh, it tastes so good that I can't eat it fast enough.

(A bone gets stuck in the wolf's throat.)

Ouch! Oh, that bone hurts my throat! I can't get it out and it's very painful! Ouch! What shall I do? I'll run down the road and perhaps I'll find someone that will help me.

(Runs down the road.)

Rabbit: What are you yelling about, Wolf?

Wolf: Oh gentle rabbit, please stick your head in my throat and pull out the bone that is choking me. Please! Please!

Rabbit: Not I, Wolf.

Wolf: I'll give you much money if you will remove the bone.

Rabbit: Not I, Wolf.

(Scampers away.)

Wolf: Someone help me! Help! Help! Help!

Donkey: What are you yelling about, Wolf?

Wolf: A bone in my throat! Please pull it out!

Donkey: Not I, Wolf.

Wolf: But I will give you much money!

Donkey: No thank you!

(Runs away.)

Wolf: Help! Help! Help!

Crane: What is wrong, Wolf?

Wolf: Oh Crane, you could really help me with your long beak. Please pull the bone out of my throat.

Aesop's Fables © 1993 Fearon Teacher Aids

Crane: Well, I don't know if I should.

Wolf: I'll give you a great deal of money if you will.

Crane: Very well, for a great deal of money I will do you the favor of pulling the bone out of your throat.

(Sticks long beak down the wolf's throat and gently pulls out the bone.)

There! Now where is the money you promised me?

Wolf: I promised you money?

Crane: Yes, you certainly did!

Wolf: Look Crane, don't ask me for money. You were lucky to get your head out of my throat without it being snapped off by my sharp teeth. Consider yourself very lucky indeed.

> **Moral:** You won't always get what you are promised.

MERCURY AND THE WORKERS

Characters: Mercury   Second Woodchopper
First Woodchopper   Neighbor

Staging: The story takes place in a forest near a deep pool. The deep pool can be several desks placed in a circle for Mercury to jump into.

First Woodchopper: Poor me! Poor me! I just dropped my wooden-handled ax into the deep pool! How will I get it out? Poor me! How will I be able to chop trees so I can make money for food? What will I do now? Alas! Poor me! Poor me!

Mercury: Stop your crying and wailing and tell me what is wrong. Perhaps I can help you.

First Woodchopper: How can you possibly help me! I just dropped my ax into the deep pool and there is no way of getting it out! Oh poor, poor me!

Mercury: Allow me to dive into the deep pool and see if I can find your ax.

(Dives into the pool and comes up holding a golden ax.)

Is this the ax you dropped into the deep pool?

First Woodchopper: No, that's not mine. Mine was not a golden ax.

Mercury: Let me try again.

(Dives into the deep pool for the second time and comes up with a silver ax.)

Is this the ax you accidentally dropped into the deep pool?

First Woodchopper: No, that's not mine, Mine was not a silver ax.

Mercury: Let me try again, woodchopper.

(Dives into the deep pool for the third time and comes up with an ax with a wooden handle.)

Is this the ax you dropped into the deep pool by accident?

First Woodchopper: Oh, yes, yes, yes! That is my ax! Thank you for finding it! Now I can chop down trees and earn money for food!

Aesop's Fables © 1993 Fearon Teacher Aids

Mercury: You are a very honest person. To reward you for your honesty, I am giving you the ax with the silver handle and the ax with the golden handle.

(Mercury suddenly disappears.)

First Woodchopper: I am rich! I am rich! I must rush home and tell my family.

(Rushes home.)

Second Woodchopper: What are you so excited about?

First Woodchopper: I dropped my wooden-handled ax into a deep pool. Mercury found it for me, but also found an ax with a silver handle and an ax with a golden handle and gave them both to me. I must now rush home to tell my family.

Second Woodchopper: How fortunate my friend is. I wish I could be as lucky.

Neighbor: Don't be so foolish! Why don't you go to the deep pool and throw in your ax and pretend it was an accident.

Second Woodchopper: That's a great idea! I'll do that now.

(Rushes to the deep pool and throws in his ax.)

Poor me! Poor me! I have just lost my ax in the deep pool. What shall I do? What shall I do?

Mercury: Why are you crying?

Second Woodchopper: I just lost my ax in the deep pool. Will you find it for me?

Mercury: I will try, woodchopper.

(Dives into the deep pool and comes up with a golden ax.)

Is this your ax with a golden handle?

Second Woodchopper: Yes! Yes! Yes! That's my ax! That's the ax I lost!

Mercury: Liar! You are a liar! And for punishment I am throwing the ax back into the deep pool and I will not get your wooden-handled ax for you!

Moral: Honesty is the best policy.

THE LION'S SHARE

Characters: Lion   Jackal
                  Fox   Wolf

Staging: The story takes place in a very deep part of a forest. When searching for food, encourage the animals to explore the entire classroom. A cardboard box can represent the prey the animals catch.

Lion: Listen, my good friends. The hunting is very poor this winter and almost every day we go hungry, right?

Fox: Very true, Lion.

Jackal: I have caught nothing for two days.

Wolf: The same is true of my efforts.

Lion: I have an excellent idea! Whenever one of us is lucky enough to catch something, we should divide it evenly with the others. This way we will all have a bit of something to eat each day.

Fox: An excellent idea!

Jackal: I agree to the plan.

Wolf: The idea sounds good to me.

Lion: Then we are all in agreement?

Fox: Right!

Jackal: Right!

Wolf: Right!

Lion: Remember, then, let us be friends as well as neighbors. Let us share evenly. Now off to the hunt!

(The animals scatter in four different directions.)

Fox: Come here, everyone! Come here! I have caught some food for us!

(All the animals come running and gather around the fox and the prey.)

Lion: Very good, Fox!

Jackal: Very good indeed, Fox!

Wolf: Well done!

Aesop's Fables © 1993 Fearon Teacher Aids

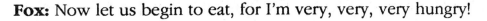

Fox: Now let us begin to eat, for I'm very, very, very hungry!

Lion: Just a moment, neighbors. Remember our agreement! There are four of us and we must divide evenly. Remember? I will now divide the food into quarters.

(Divides the prey into four equal parts.)

Jackal: Well done, Lion.

Wolf: Now let's eat, for I, too, am very, very, very hungry!

Lion: Just a moment!

Fox: What's the problem, Lion? Why should we wait?

Lion: I will explain. Now this quarter is mine as we agreed. Now this second quarter is also mine because I am a lion. This third quarter is also mine for I am stronger than all of you. And this last quarter is also mine. If any of you dare touch it, you will not leave this place alive! Any questions?

Fox: No questions, Lion.

Jackal: No questions, Lion.

Wolf: No questions from me.

Lion: Very good thinking on all your parts. Yes indeed, very good thinking!

(The lion proceeds to eat the entire dinner as the other animals watch.)

> **Moral:** Beware of empty promises.

THE FOX AND THE OLD LION

Characters: Old Lion   Rabbit
                  Fox   Jackal

Staging: The story takes place in the opening of a cave deep in a forest. The
                  opening of the cave can be two or three desks pushed together.

Old Lion: I have grown so old that I am no longer able to hunt for food. But even though I am old, I still get hungry and I need something to eat. What am I to do?

(Sits and thinks.)

I know what I will do. I'll pretend I'm very ill, and when visitors enter my cave to visit me, I'll eat them up!

(Goes deep into the cave and begins to groan and moan.)

Oh I feel so sick, so very sick! Someone come and help a poor old sick lion!

Rabbit: Are you all right in there, Lion?

Old Lion: No, little rabbit. I am very sick! Why don't you enter my cave and visit for a while.

Rabbit: Yes, I will visit with you for a while, Lion. You do look extremely ill!

(Enters the cave.)

Old Lion: Oh, I feel so very, very ill. Someone come and help a poor old sick lion!

Jackal: You sound very ill, Lion. Is there anything I can do to help you feel better?

Old Lion: Oh yes, little jackal. Come into my cave and visit for a while. I know that will cheer me up.

Jackal: Yes, I have time to visit for a short while.

(Enters the cave.)

Old Lion: Oh poor me, poor me! I'm an old sick lion and so very, very, very, ill!

Fox: You don't sound too well today, Lion.

Aesop's Fables © 1993 Fearon Teacher Aids

Old Lion: How true! How true! I feel so ill! Also I am very lonely! Won't you come into my cave and visit for a short while? It certainly would cheer me up.

Fox: I don't know if I should, Lion.

Old Lion: Why do you speak that way? Why do you hesitate?

Fox: I really don't think I should enter your cave at all!

Old Lion: Why? Why?

Fox: Well, it seems that you have had numerous visitors already by all these tracks in front of your cave, but all the tracks go only one way. I'll visit you when all the animals who have already visited you come out. Good-bye, Lion. Hope you feel better real soon!

Moral: Think for yourself.

THE SHEPHERD AND THE WOLF

Characters: Shepherd   First Neighbor
           Wolf   Second Neighbor

Staging: The story takes place in a pasture near a village.

Shepherd: I'm so bored watching these sheep. I think I will play a joke on the people of the village. Help! Help! A wolf is eating the sheep! Help! Help!

First Neighbor: I'm coming! I'm coming! Where is the wolf? I don't see a wolf!

Shepherd: Ha-ha-ha-ha-ha-ha-ha-ha! It was a joke!

First Neighbor: I don't think it was such a funny joke! I ran all the way from the village to help you. No, it was not a very funny joke!

Shepherd: I think I will try the same joke again. Help! Help! Help! Help! A wolf is eating the sheep!

Second Neighbor: I'm coming! I'm coming as fast as I can! I don't see a wolf. Are you sure you saw a wolf?

Shepherd: Ha-ha-ha-ha-ha-ha-ha-ha! It was a joke!

Second Neighbor: I don't think it was such a funny joke!

Shepherd: Ha-ha-ha-ha-ha-ha-ha-ha!

Second Neighbor: You are a foolish shepherd!

Shepherd: Ha-ha-ha-ha-ha-ha-ha! What's that noise? It's a wolf! He's going to eat my sheep! Help! Help! Help!

(A huge wolf appears.)

First Neighbor: *(from the distance)* I don't believe you.

Second Neighbor: *(from the distance)* I don't believe you, either.

Shepherd: I'm telling the truth! Help! Please help!

First Neighbor: You can't fool me again!

Second Neighbor: You can't fool me again, either!

> **Moral:** No one believes liars, even when they are telling the truth.

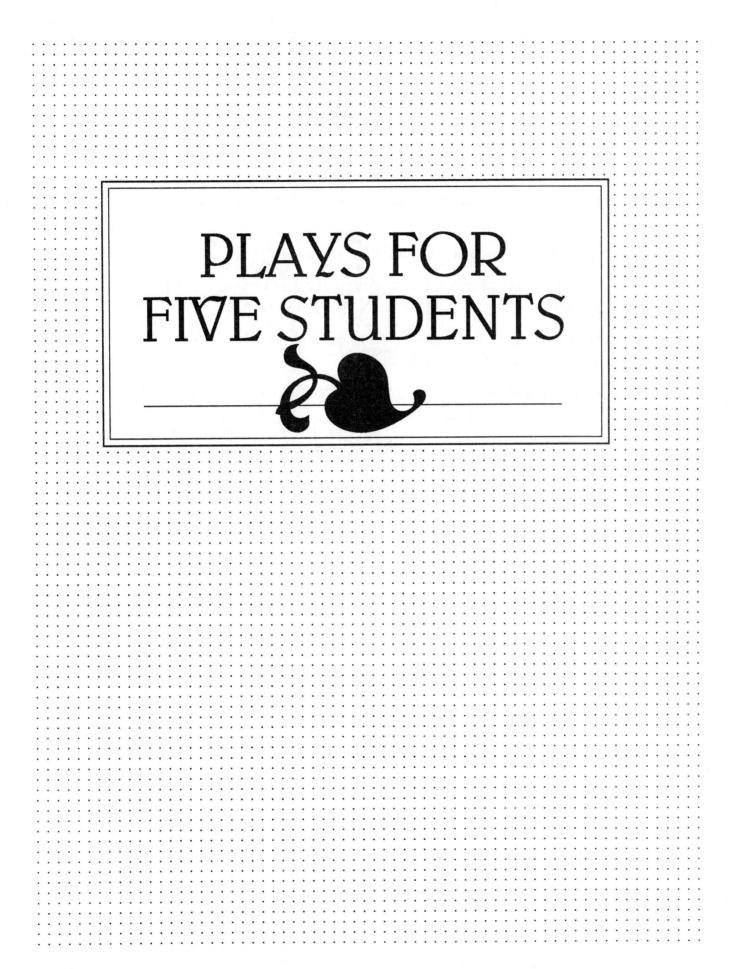

PLAYS FOR FIVE STUDENTS

THE MEETING OF THE MICE

Characters: First Mouse   Young Mouse
                 Second Mouse   Old Mouse
                 Third Mouse

Staging: The story takes place at midnight in the basement of a house. A corner of
                 the classroom can be the meeting place. Invite volunteers to be the extra
                 mice at the special meeting.

Plays for Five Students

First Mouse: What are we going to do? Oh, what are we going to do?

Second Mouse: It is a terrible situation! Yes, a terrible situation!

Third Mouse: Something has to be done about that horrible cat . . . and soon!

First Mouse: Yesterday the cat caught and ate my cousin!

Second Mouse: My best friend just barely escaped from that cat this morning!

Third Mouse: I'm so afraid of leaving my little hole!

First Mouse: I'm very much afraid, too!

Second Mouse: Me, too!

Old Mouse: Every time I want to go out for a walk, that terrible cat follows me.

Third Mouse: Well, what are we going to do about this situation?

First Mouse: I don't know. I simply don't know!

Second Mouse: I don't know, either.

(Begins to cry.)

Third Mouse: Stop crying! Your crying won't help at all!

First Mouse: I know! Let's call a special meeting of all the mice in the house. Maybe someone will have an idea about what to do about that mean old cat!

Second Mouse: Good idea!

Third Mouse: Yes! A very good idea!

Old Mouse: Maybe if we put our heads together, we can think of a way to solve this problem. That cat is becoming more dangerous every day.

Aesop's Fables © 1993 Fearon Teacher Aids

First Mouse: Listen everybody! Listen to this announcement! Everyone come out of your holes for a special meeting.

Second Mouse: Special meeting for all mice who live in this house!

Third Mouse: Hurry! Hurry! Special meeting of all mice. Now!

(All the mice gather for the special meeting.)

First Mouse: Is everyone here?

All: Yes!

First Mouse: I have called a special meeting of all the mice to see if we can figure out how to deal with the cat. Does anyone have any ideas?

Second Mouse: I don't.

Third Mouse: I don't.

Old Mouse: I don't have any ideas, either.

Young Mouse: I have an excellent idea! I know how we can deal with the cat.

First Mouse: Tell us! Tell us!

Second Mouse: Hurry and tell us!

Third Mouse: Speak up!

Old Mouse: Let's hear your idea, young mouse.

Young Mouse: Let's tie a bell around the cat's neck. The bell will warn us when the cat is coming and we can scamper away.

First Mouse: That is a wonderful idea!

Second Mouse: An excellent idea!

Third Mouse: Why didn't we think of that before!

Aesop's Fables © 1993 Fearon Teacher Aids

Old Mouse: Yes, young mouse, that is a fine idea, but there is only one problem. Who will volunteer to tie the bell around the neck of the cat?

First Mouse: Not I!

Second Mouse: Not I!

Third Mouse: Not I!

Old Mouse: Not I!

Young Mouse: And not I!

(All the mice return to their holes.)

Moral: Don't make plans unless you're willing to carry them out.

THE FARMER AND THE STORK

Characters: Farmer   Second Crane
                      Stork   Third Crane
                      First Crane

Staging: The story takes place in a cornfield. Use an imaginary net as a trap for the birds.

Farmer: I am sick and tired of those cranes that come to eat the seeds I plant every spring. This year I'm going to place a net to capture them.

(Spreads a net and then hides in the bushes to await the arrival of the cranes.)

I must be very quiet for I see four cranes flying this way. Yes, I must be quiet . . . very, very, very quiet so I won't frighten them away. And I must also be ready to spring my net to catch them all.

(The four birds come closer and closer and finally land on the field. The farmer springs the net and snares them.)

First Crane: Help! I'm trapped! Help!

Second Crane: Help! I'm trapped! Help!

Third Crane: Both my feet are trapped! Help!

Stork: Help! Help! Please let me go, Farmer. Have pity on me!

Farmer: Why should I let you go? Every year you cranes eat the seeds I plant. When harvest time comes, I have no corn and my family and I go hungry through the winter. I must stop you cranes from eating my seeds.

Stork: But can't you see that I am not a crane!

Farmer: What do you mean?

Stork: Look at my feathers. They are not like the others. Look! I'm not a crane. I'm a stork!

Farmer: But you came to my field to eat my seeds.

Stork: No! No! No! I was just passing by and paused to rest. I never eat seeds. I like fish. I'm a stork, not a crane!

Aesop's Fables © 1993 Fearon Teacher Aids

Farmer: Maybe so. Maybe so. However, all I know is that you were with the cranes who rob my fields of seeds and so you must be punished, too!

> **Moral:** Choose who you associate with wisely.

Aesop's Fables © 1993 Fearon Teacher Aids

THE LION AND THE MOUSE

Characters: Lion
                  Mouse
                  First Hunter

Second Hunter
Third Hunter

Staging: The story takes place in the lair of a sleeping lion. The lion can sleep underneath a table. The net can be imaginary.

Mouse: I see a tiny piece of food near the mighty lion's paw. Do I dare risk trying to get it? The lion seems to be sound asleep and I am very hungry! Yes, I will risk it!

(Very carefully creeps near the food. Suddenly the lion slaps its paw right down on the little mouse.)

Lion: Now I have you, my little mouse.

Mouse: Please, oh please, Lion, have mercy upon a little mouse.

Lion: Why should I? You will make a tasty morsel.

Mouse: Oh, Lion, I am so tiny. I truly am not worth eating.

Lion: Yes, you do seem to be quite tiny.

Mouse: A mighty lion, such as you, deserves a bigger mouthful.

Lion: Yes, I guess you are right. Be gone and don't enter my lair again, for next time I really will gobble you up!

Mouse: Oh, thank you, thank you, thank you! You are a very generous lion. Thank you, thank you!

Lion: Stop thanking me and get out of my lair so I can go back to sleep.

Mouse: Yes, kind Lion.

(Scampers out of the lion's lair.)

Lion: What a silly little mouse. Well, back to sleep.

(Begins to snore loudly.)

First Hunter: That lion is really sleeping soundly.

Second Hunter: Listen to the heavy snores.

Third Hunter: Do we dare risk trapping him?

First Hunter: I don't know. I don't know.

Aesop's Fables © 1993 Fearon Teacher Aids

Plays for Five Students

Second Hunter: Let's move closer and see how fast asleep the lion really is.

Third Hunter: Move very quietly!

(The three hunters slowly creep up to the entrance of the lair.)

First Hunter: Listen to those snores!

Second Hunter: That lion is snoring so loudly that it almost shakes the trees!

Third Hunter: I think we should take a chance and capture this lion. What do you think?

First Hunter: Let's try it!

Second Hunter: Get the net ready!

Third Hunter: Are we ready!

First Hunter: Yes!

Second Hunter: Yes!

Third Hunter: Let's go!

(Slowly the hunters enter the lion's lair and wrap the net around the lion.)

Lion: Help! Help! Help!

First Hunter: No sense struggling, Lion. You can't escape from our strong net.

Second Hunter: Let's rush back to the village and get some of our neighbors to help us carry the lion.

Third Hunter: Everyone in the village will be very proud of us for catching such a big strong lion.

(The hunters leave for the village.)

Lion: Help! Help! Help! Somebody help me! Help! Help!

Aesop's Fables © 1993 Fearon Teacher Aids

Mouse: That sounds like the lion's voice.

Lion: Help! Help! Help! Please help me!

Mouse: It is the lion's voice!

Lion: Help! Help! I'm trapped! Help! Help! Help!

Mouse: I'm coming Lion! I'm coming!

Lion: Oh little mouse, look at the mess I'm in. I can't get loose from this powerful net that the three hunters have cast over me. What shall I do?

Mouse: I can help you.

Lion: You can help me? How?

Mouse: With my strong sharp teeth I can gnaw a big hole in the net and then you will be able to escape.

Lion: Please try.

(The mouse gnaws and gnaws and gnaws and finally the lion is free.)

Mouse: There! I told you I could free you.

Lion: Thank you, little mouse. You really are a friend.

> **Moral:** One good deed leads to another.

Aesop's Fables © 1993 Pearon Teacher Aids

THE MULES AND THE ROBBERS

Characters: First Mule   Second Robber
                  Second Mule   Third Robber
                  First Robber

Staging: The story takes place along a country road.

First Mule: My two saddlebags are full of jewels and gold! The master chose me to carry her valuables. Poor you! All you carry in your two saddlebags is dusty grain.

Second Mule: I guess I'm not as lucky as you, but I do my job the best I can.

First Mule: I'll say you aren't lucky. I can walk with my head erect and proud and everyone notices me! Poor you! Nobody, but nobody, looks at you.

Second Mule: Yes, you are right. Nobody notices me. All I carry is two dusty bags of grain.

(Three robbers creep up to the nearby bushes.)

First Robber: Let's go over our plan again. I will jump on the proud mule and hold him tightly.

Second Robber: As you hold the proud mule, I will grab the bag of jewels.

Third Robber: And I will grab the bag of gold.

First Robber: Remember to work quickly.

Second Robber: What about the other mule?

Third Robber: No need to bother with that mule, for she is only carrying two dusty bags of grain.

First Robber: Are you ready?

Second Robber: Ready!

Third Robber: Attack!

(The three robbers carry out their plan and then run away.)

First Mule: Ouch! Poor me! Poor me! Those robbers didn't touch you at all!

Aesop's Fables © 1993 Fearon Teacher Aids

Second Mule: I guess I was the lucky one this time!

First Mule: Poor me!

> **Moral:** Too much pride can get you into trouble.

Two Travelers and a Purse

Characters: First Traveler   Second Villager
                   Second Traveler   Third Villager
                   First Villager

Staging: The story takes place on a path in the countryside.

First Traveler: Look! There is a purse in the middle of the road. It's a very heavy purse! Maybe it's full of gold! Yes! Yes! It is full of money. How lucky I am! Oh, how lucky I am!

Second Traveler: Just a moment, my friend. Don't you think you should say how lucky we are?

First Traveler: Oh no! I found it and it's all mine! Every piece of gold is mine, mine, mine!

Second Traveler: But aren't we friends? Are we not traveling together? Shouldn't we share our good fortune, as well as the bad!

First Traveler: No! No! No! I found the purse and it's all mine! Is that clear?

(Three villagers run shouting down the road.)

First Villager: Hey, you there! Stop!

Second Villager: Stop thief!

Third Villager: Help us catch the thief!

First Traveler: I'm frightened! Those people are carrying big sticks and seem very angry.

Second Traveler: Yes, they are very angry and they are carrying big clubs!

First Traveler: We are in a very bad situation! If they find the purse upon us, they will think we stole it.

Second Traveler: Just a moment! Don't say we are in a bad situation. Remember you just said that the purse was all yours. You would not say we before, so don't use the word we now!

Moral: If you share the good times with a friend, your
friend will share the bad.

Aesop's Fables © 1993 Fearon Teacher Aids

THE FOX AND THE CAT

Characters: Fox   First Hound Dog
                  Cat   Second Hound Dog
                  Hunter

Staging: The story takes place in the middle of a forest. A chair can represent a tree.

Fox: Do you know something, Cat? I'm much more clever than you are. Do you realize that?

Cat: I don't exactly know what you mean.

Fox: What I'm saying is that I know more tricks than you do.

Cat: That probably is true, for I don't know many tricks. In fact, I only know one trick.

(Sound of a hunter's horn and the barking of hound dogs.)

Fox: What was that? What was that noise?

Cat: That sounded like the horn of a hunter and the barking of hounds.

Fox: Do you suppose they are after us?

Cat: Possibly.

Fox: What shall we do?

Cat: Well, I am going to show you the only trick I know and run up this tree to safety.

(Runs up the tree.)

Fox: But I don't know how to climb trees. What shall I do, Cat?

Cat: Well, you bragged about having so many tricks. Let me see some of them.

Hunter: There's the fox standing near the tree. Catch him, my beautiful hound dogs.

(The hounds chase the fox and catch him.)

Moral: Having common sense is better than knowing many tricks.

Aesop's Fables © 1993 Fearon Teacher Aids

THE DONKEY IN THE LION'S SKIN

Characters: Donkey   Hawk
Deer   Fox
Snake

Staging: The story takes place deep in a forest. Use a blanket to drape over the
donkey to represent a lion's skin.

Donkey: Well, look what I just found! The skin of a lion! My, this must have been a big proud lion at one time. I think I will have some fun with this lion skin. I'll put it on and wander about scaring all the creatures of the forest. It will be great, great fun!

(Puts on the lion's skin and begins to frighten the creatures of the forest.)

Hello, Deer. You had better start running, for I am a wild lion and I am going to eat you up!

Deer: Oh my! I'm so frightened!

(Runs quickly away.)

Donkey: Ha-ha-ha-ha-ha-ha-ha! I certainly fooled that silly deer. Who else can I frighten?

(Looks around.)

Hello, Snake. I am a ferocious lion, and you had better crawl away as fast as you can or I will chew you up!

Snake: I'm going! I'm going!

(Crawls away quickly.)

Donkey: Ha-ha-ha-ha-ha-ha-ha! I never saw a snake crawl so fast in all my life. Ha-ha-ha-ha-ha-ha! This is great fun! I think I will now frighten Hawk. Hello, Hawk. You had better fly away quickly or I will pounce upon you and that will be the end of you!

Hawk: Good-bye Lion!

(Flies up into the sky and far away.)

Donkey: Ha-ha-ha-ha-ha-ha-ha-ha-ha-ha! Oh, my stomach hurts from laughing so much! Ha-ha-ha-ha-ha! Hello, Fox. You look so very frightened of me.

Fox: No, I'm not frightened of you! Why on earth should I be afraid?

Donkey: What do you mean? Of course you are frightened of me. I'm a wild ferocious lion. Don't you see my shaggy mane and my long tail? All the other animals in the forest are afraid of me.

Fox: I was frightened of you until you opened your big mouth. It was then that I realized you were not a ferocious lion, but simply a harmless donkey. Even though you are wearing a lion's skin, you cannot disguise the sound of your donkey voice. Good-bye, Donkey in a lion's skin.

> **Moral:** Don't pretend to be something that you aren't.

Aesop's Fables © 1993 Fearon Teacher Aids

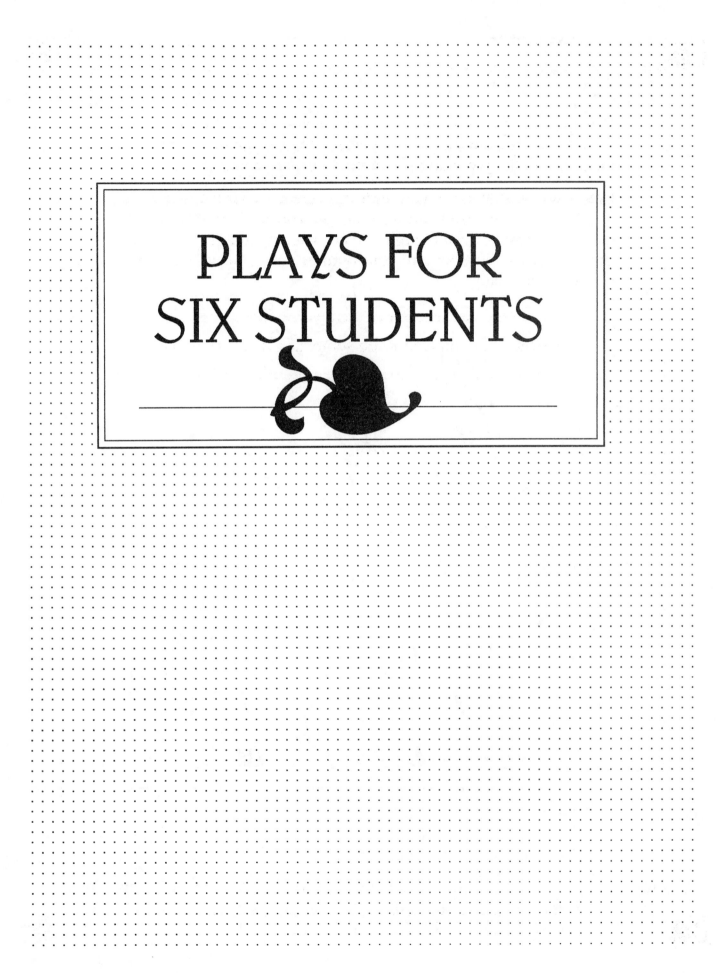

PLAYS FOR SIX STUDENTS

THE MILLER, HIS SON, AND THEIR DONKEY

Characters:	Miller	Second Woman
	His Son	First Man
	First Woman	Second Man

Staging: The story takes place along a village road leading toward a city. The miller and his son are walking beside their donkey. The donkey can be represented by a desk or a chair.

First Woman: Well, if this isn't a silly sight! I never saw two such foolish fellows as you!

Miller: What do you mean, old woman?

First Woman: Why are you two walking beside your donkey when one of you could be riding?

Miller: Thank you, old woman, for your kind advice. You ride on the mule, my son, and I will walk alongside.

Son: Yes, father.

First Man: That is a disgrace! A real disgrace!

Miller: What are you talking about, old man?

First Man: As I have always said, there is no respect shown to old age these days.

Miller: Please explain more clearly what you mean, old man.

First Man: Get off that donkey, young man, and let your poor, tired father ride!

Miller: Thank you for your advice, old man. Get off the donkey, son. You walk and I will ride.

Second Woman: I can't believe my eyes!

Miller: What is it you can't believe, old woman?

Second Woman: How do you have the nerve to ride the donkey when your poor little boy can hardly keep up?

Miller: Thank you for your advice, old woman. Get up on the donkey with me, my son.

Son: Yes, father.

Second Man: You two should be ashamed of yourselves!

Miller: What do you mean, old man!

Aesop's Fables © 1993 Fearon Teacher Aids

Second Man: I will tell you what I mean. Your poor donkey looks so tired and yet you two sit upon him with smiling faces. You both look so much stronger than your donkey that I should think it would be easier for you to carry him.

Miller: Thank you for your advice, old man.

(The miller and his son get off the donkey and carry him. After a while the donkey becomes so heavy that they accidentally drop him in the river.)

Son: Oh dear! Look what has happened to our donkey!

Miller: Poor me! Poor me! Yes, we have lost our donkey!

Moral: You can't please everybody.

Aesop's Fables © 1993 Fearon Teacher Aids

THE WOLVES AND THE SHEEP

Characters: First Wolf   Second Sheep
Second Wolf   Third Sheep
First Sheep   Dog

Staging: The story takes place in a meadow where some wolves are talking to some sheep.

First Wolf: It's silly that we can't be friends.

Second Wolf: Why is there always warfare between us?

First Sheep: Wouldn't it be nice if we really could be friends?

First Wolf: That is exactly what I'm talking about!

Second Sheep: Yes, but the dog that watches over us does not trust you, wolves.

Second Wolf: He is the one who causes all the problems.

First Wolf: He always barks at us when we come too close to you. We just want to be friendly.

Third Sheep: He barks to protect us from you.

First Wolf: Yes, the dog is to blame for placing evil thoughts in your minds.

Second Wolf: We don't want to harm you. All we want is your friendship.

First Sheep: Perhaps what you say is true.

First Wolf: Of course, we are telling the truth.

Second Sheep: Well, tell us then what we should do.

Second Wolf: The best thing for you to do is to tell the dog to go home and that you don't need him anymore.

First Wolf: If we are going to be friends, why do you need a dog to protect you?

Third Sheep: That makes sense to me.

Second Wolf: Go ahead and tell the dog to go home.

First Sheep: Dog! Dog! Go home. We don't need you anymore.

Dog: Are you sure?

Aesop's Fables © 1993 Fearon Teacher Aids

Second Sheep: Yes, we are sure! Go home!

Third Sheep: Go home! Go home! Go home!

(The dog wanders home. As soon as the dog is out of sight, the wolves pounce upon the sheep and gobble them up.)

> **Moral:** Be careful who you trust.

THE FOX WHO LOST HIS TAIL

Characters: Red Fox   Black Fox
Brown Fox   White Fox
Gray Fox   Old Fox

Staging: The story begins with Red Fox catching his tail in a trap. Encourage the foxes to come from all directions in the classroom for the special meeting.

Red Fox: Oh, dear, my tail is caught in a trap. What am I to do? Someone come and help me before the hunter returns. Help! Help! Help! What am I to do? I guess the only thing I can do now is pull and pull and pull and hope I can free my tail.

(Pulls and pulls and pulls until freed.)

At last I am free! But, oh poor me! I have lost my tail. I look so silly without a tail. All my friends will laugh at me. What shall I do? I'll call a meeting of all the foxes.

(Begins to yell.)

Attention all foxes of the forest! Special meeting today of all foxes!

(All the foxes gather for the meeting.)

Brown Fox: I think we are all here, Red Fox.

Red Fox: Then I will tell you why I called this special meeting.

Gray Fox: Hurry and tell us.

White Fox: I am very curious.

Red Fox: I wanted to tell you what a happy fox I am without a tail.

Black Fox: Are you really happy not having a tail, Red Fox? I must say you look rather strange without a tail.

Red Fox: Oh, yes, Black Fox, I am very, very happy without a tail.

White Fox: Can you tell us why, Red Fox?

Red Fox: Certainly I can.

Old Fox: Well begin, for we are all interested and listening.

Red Fox: Well, first of all, I can move about much easier now. Look how easily I turn around. You should try to lose your tails and be as lucky as I am!

(Shows the other foxes how easily it is to move about.)

Brown Fox: You do that very well, Red Fox.

Gray Fox: Yes, very well indeed.

White Fox: You do seem to move easily without a tail.

Old Fox: Give us another reason why we should attempt to lose our tails and be like you. I'm still not convinced.

Red Fox: Why, without a tail, it is much easier to creep through holes and jump over fences to get away from the hounds.

Black Fox: That could be very true.

Brown Fox: There is something to what you say.

Gray Fox: I agree that a tail can be a nuisance sometimes.

Red Fox: And, of course, without a tail there is less chance of getting caught in a trap.

White Fox: Like you did?

Red Fox: Exactly as I did.

Old Fox: You give us many reasons why we should remove our tails, but I don't believe you, Red Fox.

Red Fox: What are you talking about, Old Fox?

Old Fox: If you had a chance to get your tail back, you wouldn't be so interested in urging us to lose our tails. No, Red Fox, you can't fool me, and I don't think you will be able to fool the other foxes either.

> **Moral:** To convince someone, you must believe in what you are saying.

Aesop's Fables © 1993 Fearon Teacher Aids

Plays for Six Students

THE SICK STAG

Characters: Sick Stag   Fox
                    Jackal   Raven
                    Rat   Ox

Staging: The story takes place in a corner of a pasture where the sick stag is resting surrounded by food that has been left to help him get well.

Jackal: Hello, Stag, I just dropped by to see how you are feeling.

Stag: Not too well. Not too well, I'm afraid. But it was nice of you to come by and visit.

Jackal: It's the least a friend can do. My, isn't that a tasty bit of meat you have there. Do you mind if I taste it? It looks so good!

Stag: You may taste it.

Jackal: Thank you, I will!

(Eats up all the meat.)

Well, I hope you feel better soon. Good-bye.

Rat: Hello, Stag. I just dropped by to see how you are feeling.

Stag: Not too well. Not too well, I'm afraid. However, it was nice of you to drop by for a visit.

Rat: It's the least a friend can do. My, isn't that a nice piece of cheese you have there. Do you mind if I just take a tiny taste? It looks so nice and soft.

Stag: You may taste the cheese.

Rat: Thank you, I will.

(Eats up all the cheese.)

Well, I hope you feel better soon, Stag. Good-bye.

Fox: Hello, Stag. I just dropped by to see how you were feeling.

Stag: Not too well. Not too well, I'm afraid. However, it was very nice of you to drop by and visit.

Fox: It's the least a friend can do. I'm so thirsty and your water looks so deliciously cool. Do you mind if I just take a small sip?

Aesop's Fables © 1993 Fearon Teacher Aids

Stag: You may have a sip.

Fox: Thank you, I will.

(Laps up all the water.)

Well, I hope you feel better soon. Good-bye.

Raven: Hello! I just dropped by to see how you are feeling.

Stag: Not too well. Not too well, I'm afraid. But it was very nice of you to come by and visit.

Raven: It's the least a friend can do. Say, those berries you have there certainly look bright and juicy. Do you mind if I eat one of your berries?

Stag: You may have a berry.

Raven: Thank you, I will.

(Gobbles up all the berries.)

Hope you will be better soon. Good-bye!

Ox: I just dropped by to see how you are feeling.

Stag: Not too well. Not too well, I'm afraid. However, it was most kind of you to take the time to come to visit.

Ox: It's the least a friend can do. Say, that straw you are resting on looks so fresh and clean. Do you mind if I have a small taste?

Stag: You may have a mouthful of the straw.

Ox: Thank you, I will.

(Eats up all the straw the stag is resting upon.)

I hope you feel better very soon. Good-bye.

Stag: All my friends came to visit, and now I am left with absolutely nothing . . . no food, no water, and not even my straw to rest upon.

> **Moral:** A person who says he or she is a friend should act like a friend.

Aesop's Fables © 1993 Fearon Teacher Aids

THE MILK WOMAN AND HER PAIL

Characters: Milk Woman   Third Stranger
                   First Stranger   Fourth Stranger
                   Second Stranger   Fifth Stranger

Staging: The story takes place along a country road. A book balanced on the milk woman's head can represent a pail of milk. When the milk woman meets the five strangers, they should be in various parts of the room.

First Stranger: Where are you going, woman, with that pail of milk on your head?

Milk Woman: I am going to market to sell my milk, and with the money, I am going to buy three hundred eggs.

First Stranger: Good luck!

Milk Woman: Thank you.

Second Stranger: Where are you going, woman, with that pail of milk on your head?

Milk Woman: I am going to market to sell my milk, and with the money, I am going to buy three hundred eggs and those three hundred eggs will become three hundred chickens.

Second Stranger: Good luck!

Milk Woman: Thank you.

Third Stranger: Where are you going, woman, with that pail of milk on your head?

Milk Woman: I am going to market to sell my milk, and with the money, I will buy three hundred eggs that will become three hundred chickens. Then I will sell the three hundred chickens and buy myself a pretty new gown.

Third Stranger: Good luck to you!

Milk Woman: Thank you, stranger.

Fourth Stranger: Where are you going, woman, with that pail of milk on your head?

Milk Woman: I am going to market to sell my milk for money, and with the money, I will buy three hundred eggs that in time will become three hundred chickens. Then I will sell the three hundred chickens for a pretty new gown to wear to the Christmas party!

Fourth Stranger: Good luck to you!

Aesop's Fables © 1993 Fearon Teacher Aids

Plays for Six Students

Milk Woman: Thank you, stranger.

Fifth Stranger: Where are you going, woman, with that pail of milk on your head?

Milk Woman: I am going to market to sell my milk for money, and with the money, I will buy three hundred eggs that in time will become three hundred chickens. Then I will sell the three hundred chickens for a pretty new gown to wear to the Christmas party!

Fifth Stranger: Well, you certainly have many plans.

Milk Woman: Yes, I do! And when I am at the Christmas party and all the guests ask "Is that a new dress?" I will shake my head "Yes!" I will shake my head just like this!

(Shakes her head and the milk pail falls to the ground.)

Moral: Big plans are sometimes hard to accomplish.

THE SHOEMAKER TURNED DOCTOR

Characters: Shoemaker   Third Villager
                   First Villager   Fourth Villager
                   Second Villager   Fifth Villager

Staging: The story takes place in a small village.

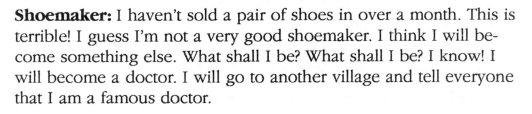

Shoemaker: I haven't sold a pair of shoes in over a month. This is terrible! I guess I'm not a very good shoemaker. I think I will become something else. What shall I be? What shall I be? I know! I will become a doctor. I will go to another village and tell everyone that I am a famous doctor.

(Locks up the store and walks to another village.)

First Villager: Someone told me you were a famous doctor. Is that true?

Shoemaker: Yes, very true. I am a famous doctor.

Second Villager: What makes you such a famous doctor?

Third Villager: I never heard of you before. How come you say you are famous?

Shoemaker: Listen, my friends, and I will tell you. I have invented a medicine that will cure you if you ever are poisoned!

Fourth Villager: Is that really true?

Shoemaker: Absolutely true, my friend.

First Villager: I will buy a bottle of your medicine.

Second Villager: I will buy a bottle, too.

Third Villager: Me, too!

Fourth Villager: Are you sure it works?

Shoemaker: Absolutely sure! Why, only last week I cured a woman who was bitten by a poisonous snake. My medicine cured her in two minutes!

Fourth Villager: Really! I will buy two bottles!

First Villager: I will take another bottle!

Second Villager: Me, too.

Third Villager: Give me another bottle, too.

Shoemaker: Sorry, my friends, I have just sold the last bottle, but I will be back tomorrow with more.

(All the villagers leave for their homes. A scorpion comes along and bites the shoemaker.)

Shoemaker: Help! Help! Help! I have just been bitten by a scorpion. I have been poisoned. Help! Help!

Fifth Villager: Well, well, well, our famous doctor is sick. Here! Drink some of your own medicine and be cured.

Shoemaker: No! No! No! My medicine will make me worse. I am not really a doctor. I was just pretending.

> **Moral:** When you don't tell the truth, you usually get caught.

Aesop's Fables © 1993 Fearon Teacher Aids

THE ARCHER AND THE MOUNTAIN LION

Characters: Rabbit   Mountain Lion
                  Deer   Archer
                  Snake   Fox

Staging: The story takes place in the mountains. Encourage the archer to create a
                  sound to give the impression of an arrow flying through the air.

Rabbit: Beware, everyone! Here comes the archer. I'm leaving!

Deer: The archer is a very dangerous hunter. Beware, everyone.

Snake: Everyone, beware, and get out of here for the archer is within striking distance.

Mountain Lion: I am not going to leave. I will stay and challenge the hunter.

Snake: You are a very foolish mountain lion. You are wasting your time challenging an archer.

Mountain Lion: Why? Tell me why!

Snake: You will find out soon enough mountain lion.

(The snake and all the other animals run away.)

Mountain Lion: Here I am, archer, and I am not afraid of you! I am staying right where I am!

Archer: Very well, mountain lion, I will send you a messenger. It will tell you how dangerous I am!

(Shoots an arrow at the mountain lion and narrowly misses.)

Mountain Lion: Help! Help! That arrow almost hit me. I, too, am leaving here.

Fox: Don't run away, mountain lion. Be brave and stay. Face the archer again.

Mountain Lion: I am not listening to your advice. If the archer can send such a dangerous messenger, imagine how dangerous the archer must be.

Moral: Beware of a person who can hurt you.

Aesop's Fables © 1993 Fearon Teacher Aids